Growing Chilies
A Beginners Guide to Growing, Using and Surviving Chilies

Jason Johns

No part of this publication may be replicated, redistributed, or given away in any form without the prior written consent of the author/publisher.

Visit me at www.GardeningWithJason.com for gardening tips and advice or follow me at www.YouTube.com/OwningAnAllotment for my video diary and tips. Join me on Facebook at www.Facebook.com/OwningAnAllotment.

Follow me on Instagram and Twitter as @allotmentowner for regular updates, news, offers and information on all aspects of gardening.

If you have enjoyed this book, please leave a review.

© 2022 Jason Johns

All rights reserved.

TABLE OF CONTENTS

Introducing The Chilli 3
A Brief History of Chillies 5
Handling Chilies Safely 7
The Anatomy of the Chilli 9
Chilli Cultivars 11
    Capsicum Annuum 12
    Capsicum Chinense 14
    Capsicum Frutescens 16
    Capsicum Baccatum 18
    Capsicum Pubescens 19
    Popular Chilli Varieties 21
    Popular Chillies by Heat Level 43
The Scoville Scale Explained 46
    What Is Capsaicin? 48
Health Benefits of Chillies 52
Before You Start Growing Chillies 57
    Equipment Needed 57
    Where to Buy Seeds 59
    Can I Grow Chillies Where I Live? 59
    Growing Indoors vs. Outdoors 60
    Tips for Growing Chillies in Cooler Climates 61
How to Grow Chilli Plants 63
    Sowing & Germinating Your Seeds 63
    Transplanting Your Chilli Plants 66
    Caring for Your Plants 68
        Light Requirements 69
        Temperature Requirements 70
        Fertilising 71
        Watering 74
    Pruning 77
    How To Make Chillies Hotter 78
Growing Chillies In A Greenhouse 81
Harvesting Chillies 83
Saving Your Chilli Seeds 85
Overwintering Chilli Plants 89
Growing Chillies in Containers 91
Growing Chillies in a Hydroponic Environment 94
    Hydroponic Growing Methods 95
    Lighting Requirements 100
    Growing the Plants 101
Ornamental Chilli Varieties 104

Pests, Diseases, and Problems 108
   Diagnosing Problems 109
   Common Chilli Pests 111
      Insect Pests 111
      Common Chilli Diseases 115
      Viral Diseases 118
   Common Chilli Problems 119
Frequently Asked Questions 121
Breeding Your Own Chilli Varieties 124
Making Chilli Sauces 130
   Fermenting Chillies 131
   Chilli Sauce Recipes 133
How to Dry Chillis 141
Making a Chilli Ristra 143
Smoking Chillies 145
Pickling Chillies 147
Making A Chilli Oil 150
Freezing Chillies 152
How to Make Chilli Powder 154
Recipes for Chillies 156
Endnote 170
About Jason 173
Other Books By Jason 175
Want More Inspiring Gardening Ideas? 182
Free Book! 182

Chapter 1

An Introduction to Growing Chillies

Introducing The Chilli

Chillies, or chilies, depending on where in the world you are from, are a spicy vegetable that has grown in popularity over the last decade or so. Once solely the remit of Mexican or Indian food, chillies are now used in many different cuisines as they have a wide range of flavours, from mild to fruity to sweet to burning hot. They have developed a very popular niche market and an entire industry has built around hot sauces and hot chillies.

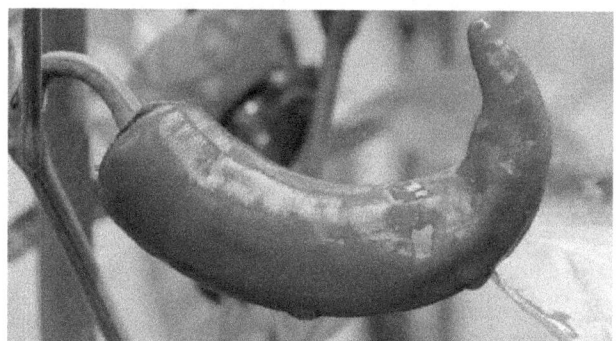

More and more varieties of chilli have been bred, ranging from the cool and flavoursome to the wickedly hot Carolina Reaper that most people regret instantly when eaten. It has become very competitive to grow the hottest chilli with new plants being submitted for consideration every year. However, chillies are not necessarily just hot, some of them have a subtle flavour that is delicious. Many people get obsessed with the need to grow super-hot chillies, not realising that some of the milder varieties lend incredible flavours to your cooking and are much more palatable.

Whichever variety you grow, they all require pretty much the same care and attention. It is the length of the growing season that is important, as the chilli plant comes from South America and requires quite a long time to mature and produce fruit. Chilli plants are not annuals, which many people in northern climates believe, and can be overwintered in a protected environment so they continue to grow, producing fruit, the following year.

This book introduces you to chillies and shows you exactly how to grow them. You will be walked through selecting varieties, though I cannot detail all the different varieties here as there are over 4,000 different known varieties, but I will talk about the more popular and commonly grown types. You learn how to germinate seeds, transplant your chillies and look after them as they grow.

As well as this, you will learn how to keep your plants healthy, avoiding some of the common mistakes people make when growing these plants.

Once you have grown the chillies you need to harvest and store them. We'll talk about the many different ways you can store your chillies, including drying them for later use as well as some of my favourite recipes involving this interesting fruit. They are fantastic used in cooking, and you can use whichever type of chilli you want to get the heat level you want.

Remember when eating chillies that if they are too hot and your mouth is burning, you should avoid water or alcohol, but instead drink milk or a dairy product as this neutralises the burning sensation. Water or alcohol does nothing to cool your mouth down, so if you are trying some super-hot chillies, make sure you have a large glass of milk to hand.

Enjoy growing your chillies at home, but before we continue, here's a little history lesson as you look into the origins of this popular plant.

A Brief History of Chillies

Chillies have become one of the most popular spices in the world, used in a wide variety of dishes. They are one of the few spices that were taken from the Americas to the New World, with most spices having come from the Far East.

Chillies are members of the Capsicum genus, which are all members of the deadly nightshade (*Solanaceae*) family. Capsicum range from the sweet bell or pointed peppers that are crunchy and enjoyed in salads to the dangerously hot Naga and Carolina Reaper chillies, which are so hot you shouldn't even handle them without wearing gloves.

Chillies originate in the Americas where they were cultivated by the native people for at least the last 7,500 years. As they are high in vitamin C, they increase the uptake of non-red blood cell iron in diets that do not contain a great deal of meat. The Mesoamerican diet relied heavily on beans and maize, so chillies would have been crucial in providing flavour and vitamins.

Although Columbus landed in the Americas in 1492, he didn't bring back the chilli from that voyage, though he did write about a type of pepper that the natives used. It was in 1498 that the Portuguese brought the chilli back to their homeland, the Cape Verde islands and into West Africa. In particular, they brought the Piri-Piri pepper, which was naturalised in West Africa and now grows wild in the area. For this reason, it is often thought of as being native to this continent even though it is not.

Over the coming years, the chilli spread towards the east along the Silk Road, into India, China and by 1549 it made it to Japan.

At this time, spices were considered very valuable, and much of the trade was based around these expensive commodities. Chillies were extremely popular because they provided the heat of black pepper without any bitterness associated with some other spices. The fresh chilli provided a lot of flavour, whereas the dried chilli could be used for heat but without the flavour of the raw fruit.

The chemical capsaicin is responsible for the heat in chillies, which has hydrophobic properties, so water does not reduce the burning. This burning chemical buries itself into the surfaces of your mouth, and causes the irritation. The burning sensation is actually to deter animals from eating the plant, but us humans think it is tasty and fun, or at least some of us do Foods that are rich in fat such as milk and yogurt eliminate capsaicin and stop the burning. This is why you often see yogurt and yogurt-based dips served as side dishes in Indian cuisine, where the chilli is a frequent addition.

Oddly enough, it wasn't until the latter half of the 1800's that Europeans realised that chillies came from the Americas. You will notice many chillies bear names that indicate they originated in Africa, even though the original plants were brought back from the New World by explorers. The Africans wholeheartedly adopted the chilli to the point that the fallacy of this plant originated there was spread.

Today, chillies are popular across the globe, being a staple part of many cuisines. From subtle flavour to fiery heat, chillies are a wonderful addition to many dishes.

HANDLING CHILIES SAFELY

Everyone thinks that they are fine handling chillies and that no precautions need taking. We all do it, but it only takes you rubbing a hand with chilli juice over your eyes, in your ear, up your nose or near any other sensitive area of your body and you very quickly realise why people say be careful handling chillies. Trust me when I say it is only something you do once!

The capsaicinoids in chillies are incredibly hot, and some people are more sensitive than others to them. Store bought chillies don't tend to be too hot, but you still do not want to get the juices anywhere sensitive. Home-grown super-hot chillies are positively dangerous by comparison and you will regret getting their juices anywhere on your body. Be very careful not to touch any other surfaces while preparing hot chillies as you can inadvertently transfer the burning juice to those surfaces.

With store-bought chillies, you can usually get away without wearing gloves, but wash your hands thoroughly immediately afterward. If you are sensitive to chillies, then you should wear thin rubber gloves.

With home-grown chillies, you should always take precautions, particularly as the strength starts to climb up the Scoville scale, which measures how hot the chillies are. With any of the hotter chilli varieties, don't even touch the seeds or plants with your bare hands because they are so hot.

Once you have finished preparing the chillies, wash all the utensils they have touched and the cutting board using hot, soapy water. I personally wash them twice and then put them in the dishwasher just to be sure there is no chilli juice left. You do not forget the time you touched a sensitive area of your body with hands coated in burning chilli juice.

Don't think that drying chillies makes them less dangerous. Be careful handling these as well as they are still hot. If you are grinding chillies, then be extra careful because even the fumes can be dangerous. Do not breathe them in or let them get into your eyes.

The capsaicin is concentrated in the membranous ribs of the pepper, rather than the seeds. However, the seeds are also hot because of their proximity to the ribs. If you are cooking with the chillies, you can leave the seeds in the dish for a bit of extra fire or remove them for a milder version.

Chillies are extremely hot and are extremely painful if you get them in any sensitive area, seriously, do not even go to the toilet without washing your hands thoroughly after handling them. Be very careful not to get any chilli juice in your eyes as the hotter varieties could blind you. Saying that though, they are delicious in meals and well worth using.

THE ANATOMY OF THE CHILLI

The chilli is a very simple plant made up of a number of parts as shown in the picture below. The placenta is the hottest part of the chilli as it contains the capsaicin glands. If you remove this part before use, even with the hotter chilli peppers, it does make them a little milder. For more of a kick from your chillies, leave the placenta and the seeds in place when using them.

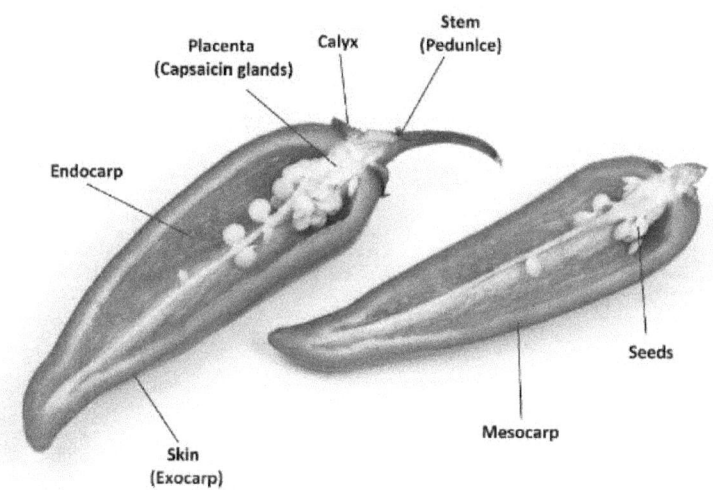

Typically, the tip of a chilli is the mildest part, and if you cut the pepper before the seeds start, then you will get the coolest parts of the chilli, but bear in mind they will still be hot on a hot chilli. All of the fruit on a single plant will not have the same heat level. Some fruits will be hotter than others, so be careful as many a person has been caught out when they suddenly find a much hotter chilli on what they thought was a mild plant.

The riper the fruit, the hotter it is in most cases, though there are some varieties which become milder as they mature. The temperature of the growing environment also influences the heat of the fruit as does the amount of water the plant is provided. When grown in a temperate climate, the fruit tends to be milder than when grown in a hot environment.

CHILLI CULTIVARS

Having originated in the south of Brazil and the eastern parts of Bolivia, the plant was spread across the Americas by birds and human activity. Due to the value of spices at the time of their discovery by Europeans, they were brought back across the Atlantic Ocean and spread across Europe, Africa, and Asia.

Today, chillies and their varieties are grown all over the world commercially and by home gardeners. It is one of the most widely cultivated crops in the world with somewhere over 4,000 different cultivars, not all of which are available commercially in all areas of the world. The entire list of chillies would make a book in itself, though the most popular cultivars include cayenne, jalapeño, poblano, habanero, bird's eye and Serrano, many of which you will have heard of and can buy in your local supermarkets. More unusual varieties can be found in local ethnic stores that provide food for the local markets. Here you can find some very interesting varieties of peppers, including some of the very hot varieties.

There are five main species of chilli, all of which will be discussed in more detail shortly:

- *Capsicum Annuum*
- *Capsicum Chinense*
- *Capsicum Pubescens*
- *Capsicum Baccatum*
- *Capsicum Frutescens*

Each of these contains a wide variety of plants with fruits of all sorts of sizes, colours, shapes, and strength! The hottest chillies fall under the Capsicum Chinense variety.

Capsicum Annuum

This is the most commonly grown type of chilli, both at home and commercially. It contains many of the best-known varieties of chilli including jalapeño, poblano, bell peppers, cayenne, Anaheim, Hungarian wax and more.

The Latin, *Annuum*, comes from the term for annual and is somewhat misleading as chillies are perennials under ideal growing conditions. They are grown as annuals across most of Europe and North America purely because the cold weather kills the plant. This family of chillies has the widest variety of shapes. The easiest way to recognise a member of this family is by the fact that they don't have any defining characteristics. All of the other species do have some characteristic traits, so any chilli that does not have those particular characteristics is a member of the *Annuum* family.

This family was split into two separate categories, hot and sweet. However, with modern breeding, there are now sweet jalapeño peppers and some varieties of hot bell peppers. Typically, we call any variety that is hot a chilli, while the sweet varieties are always referred to as bell peppers, sweet peppers, or by their colour, i.e., red, green, yellow or orange peppers.

Physical Characteristics

The pods of the *Annuum* species can be virtually any colour. When unripe, they range from red through to orange, yellow and even a brownish black colour. When ripe, the colour changes to violet, green, almost white or very nearly black. The sheer variety of colour makes this variety a colourful addition to any greenhouse or polytunnel.

Many of the colourful ornamental chilli cultivars are members of this family.

Habitat and Growing Conditions

This species evolved, according to archaeological research, in southern Brazil and Bolivia where they were domesticated around 6,100 years ago.

Like most chilli plants, this family does not tolerate very cold conditions, though it can tolerate a variety of weather. It is very productive in warm, dry climates similar to those it originated in, which means most of us will have to grow them under glass if we want a chance of a harvest

This variety grows as a perennial, but it needs temperatures of between 15°C/60°F and 29°C/85°F throughout the year.

Culinary Uses

Hot chilli peppers are used in a wide variety of cuisines, from Thai to Indian to Chinese to African and Latin American. They are used either fresh or dried or added as crushed flakes. They are used in everything from curries to stir fries and more, though often made into sauces which are used in dishes or on the side. The sweet peppers are also used in a wide variety of dishes, but often enjoyed raw in a salad, something few will do with a hot chilli pepper.

Growing Tips

The seeds for *Capsicum annuum* germinate best when planted indoors or under glass about eight to ten days before the last frost. The seeds prefer temperatures of between 21°C/70°F and 27°C/80°F. Either start the seeds off under lights or on a sunny windowsill. The seeds will not germinate if regularly exposed to temperatures below 13°C/55°F. Try to keep the seeds at temperatures above 18°C/65°F for the best results. You will get the best germination rates when the temperature is kept at a consistent level. If the temperature varies too much, such as when heat lamps go off on a cold night, germination will suffer.

The plants need plenty of light to grow strong. Be careful where you plant them as they can grow leggy if they have to reach towards a light source which puts the plant at a big disadvantage. Most people will start their chillies off under lights or in a greenhouse where they are getting consistent light. They tend to grow leggy if they have to 'reach' for the light, i.e., on a windowsill where they do not get consistent light.

Capsicum plants are a member of the same family as aubergines (eggplant) and potatoes, meaning they are susceptible to some of the same diseases. If you are planting chilli plants outdoors, avoid planting them near these other plants or where they were grown in the previous growing season.

Water the seeds once planted, then water once a week, keeping the soil damp, but not wet until the seedling is visible. Once the seed has germinated, water once every two weeks. Be careful not to over water as this will harm the seed/seedling and can cause them to rot.

These are a hard type of chilli to grow, and germination can be tricky, but the plant is rewarding. It will take around 120 days from planting for the fruit to be ready, though this does depend on the variety. The mature fruits are firm when squeezed and will store in your refrigerator for up to three weeks. You can freeze them or store them using any of the other methods detailed later in this book. If you own a heated propagator, then it will make germination much easier. If you are serious about growing chillies, then investing in one or more heated propagator will give you a much higher chance of successful germination.

Alternatively, if you do not want to germinate seeds yourself, many of these plants can be bought part grown from nurseries or specialist suppliers. While the selection will not be as large as if you were buying seeds, you are bound to find something you want to grow and it takes away from the uncertainty of germination.

Capsicum Chinense

This variety is often referred to as the "Yellow Lantern Chilli" and is famed for producing some of the hottest varieties of chilli including Trinidad Scorpion, Scotch Bonnet, Habanero, Red Savina, Congo Pepper, Jamaican Hot and many others.

Although there is some variation on the shape and size of the pods on this variety, they do all have one thing in common. They are characterised by a very definite fruity aroma which is similar to apricots.

The Latin name, *'Chinense'* translates as 'from China,' but this is obviously a misnomer. This species originated in the Amazon and is native to Central America, the Yucatan region, and the Caribbean Islands, having been traded centuries ago by European explorers with their oriental counterparts.

Popular with chilli-heads, these peppers are prized for the fiery yet fruity flavour. They are popular in Mexican and Caribbean cooking, where they give the dishes the hot kick and strong flavour these cuisines are renowned for.

While many of the varieties are volcano hot, there are some varieties which are milder and more aromatic such as Trinidad Perfume and Nu Mex Suave. If you want milder chillies with a fruiter flavour, then these cultivars are worth a try.

Physical Characteristics
Chinense plants are usually bushy with upright, rigid stems and large, thin green leaves that are wrinkly. They produce small, white flowers with five petals and typically two to six flowers per knot.

The size and shape of the peppers vary significantly and can be small and round, long and thin, bell-shaped, lantern-shaped or bonnet shaped. The chillies can be harvested any time after they form. The immature chillies are green, but as they mature they change colour, which can be anything from yellow to orange to red to purple to brown and black.

Inside the chilli you will see a spongy ribbing that divides up the inside of the pepper. There are some small, round and flat seeds internally.

Growing Tips
As a tropical species, the *Chinense* varieties prefer high humidity levels. In warm areas, this is a perennial plant and will live for some years. However, in

colder climates it cannot survive the winter outside and much be brought inside otherwise it will die.

The seeds take longer to germinate than some other species, though are not too difficult to get to sprout. Like most chilli varieties, these are best grown under glass or indoors in temperate climates otherwise they can take some time for the fruits to mature. In cooler climates, there is often not enough warm days outside for the fruit to mature fully before the growing season ends. Depending on the cultivar you are growing, the fruits are ready to harvest in between 80 and 120 days.

The heat from these chillies can be very intense so they are best kept away from pets and children as they can burn the skin, eyes, and mouth. If you are growing these as ornamental varieties and own a dog, make sure it doesn't eat them as it will hurt your pet.

Culinary Uses
These peppers are very popular in Mexican and Caribbean cuisine where they add the famed heat to the dishes. They are used in stews or as marinades or sauces.

The fruity flavour of these chilli peppers makes them essential for many of the classic dishes from these regions. As they have this fruity characteristic, replacing them with other varieties of chilli completely changes the flavour of the dish.

As these varieties tend to be extremely hot, they are popular in restaurants as a method of reducing costs. One *Chinense* chilli in a large dish can provide the same amount of heat as a number of milder chillies.

Capsicum Frutescens

The *frutescens* family of chillies isn't a large family, but it does contain probably the most famous chilli pepper of all, the Tabasco pepper. It contains others that you may have heard of, including the Piri Piri pepper, Thai pepper, and the Malawian pepper.

The origin of this species isn't very clear, though these peppers were brought to Africa where they have been naturalised, hence the names of many of the peppers in this family. It is believed that this chilli pepper originated in Central or South America, though now grows all across the Americas. It was brought to Africa by explorers who found an environment where this prized (and very valuable) spice could be grown and brought back to Europe with far less risk than a trip across the Atlantic Ocean.

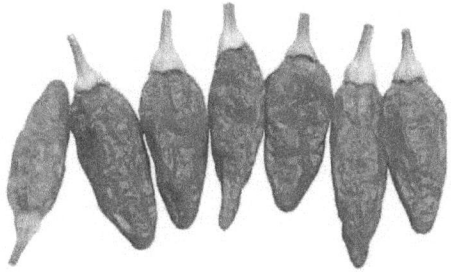

Dried Tabasco chillies

Physical Characteristics
There is very little variation in the pods of the *Frutescens* variety. The stem grows straight up and curves just before it meets the flower head. The plants tend to be quite compact, growing no more than four feet tall. As these plants are short and shrubby, they are ideal for growing in containers where they will produce a lot of flowers and fruit. A single plant can produce more than a hundred pods.

The pods are typically small and grow erect from the stalks. They are usually ellipsis-conical or lanceoloid in shape. The flowers are white with a green/yellow or green/white corolla. The immature fruits are yellow, and as they mature, they darken through a variety of shades until they become a lovely red colour.

A Tabasco chilli pepper

Culinary Uses
These chillies are popular in many African cuisines, notable Moroccan, Ethiopian and Egyptian. Of course, it most famous chilli, the Tabasco pepper, is used to make Tabasco sauce.

The Piri Piri chilli, coming from the Swahili word for pepper, goes by a variety of names including the African Devil and is popular in many cuisines from the southern parts of the African continent. This particular variety of chilli is popular as a marinade and is extensively used for chicken, particularly in restaurants such as the well-known chain Nandos.

Although popular in cooking, members of this family are often grown as ornamental plants due to their compact size and colourful fruits.

Growing Tips
Like most other chillies, these varieties like hot, humid weather, though they are not drought tolerant. They grow best in moist, well-drained soil that has been enriched with organic matter and is very fertile. If you are growing these plants outside, then do not transplant them to their final growing position until the soil has warmed and the risk of frost has completely passed. These plants do not tolerate cold weather. Grow in full sun for the plants to produce a good harvest.

Capsicum Baccatum

Members of the *baccatum* family are typically reasonable hot chillies, ranging from 30,000 to 50,000 on the Scoville scale. *Baccatum* translates from the Latin as 'berry-like,' and many members of this family produce small, compact pods, though some varieties produce longer, elongated pods.

This plant is native to Peru and Bolivia, though is grown throughout Latin America. Some of the best-known cultivars are Bishop's Crown, Lemon Drop, Wild Baccatum and Brazilian Starfish. The fruits of this plant have a unique shape which is similar to tulip flowers.

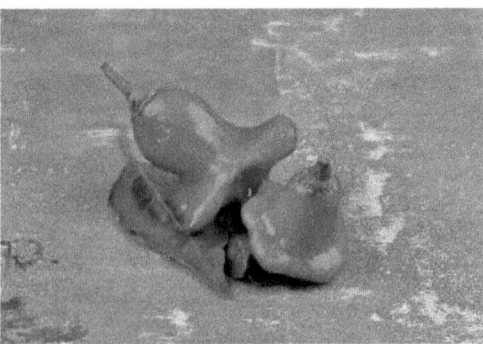
Bishop's Crown chilli peppers

These chillies have a smoky and fruity flavour that is very distinct and not found in any other chilli variety. The heat levels can vary from mild to burning hot. It has a complex taste that is not overpowering as the wings of these chillies tend to be mild and sweet, despite the heat of the chilli. They are unique and have yet to become popular outside of Latin America, meaning they may be difficult to obtain from anywhere other than a specialist supplier.

Physical Characteristics

Baccatum translates from Latin as 'berry-like,' which gives you an idea of the appearance of the fruits. Typically, they are an inch or two high and two to three inches across. The chillies mature into wrinkled, colourful pods that range from yellow to orange and red.

The plants grow up to five feet tall and spread to around three feet wide. The young pods are erect and as they mature they become more pendant, making for a good-looking, ornamental plant.

Culinary Uses

These chillies, and particularly the Aji Amarillo chilli, are strongly associated with Peruvian and Bolivian cuisines. In Bolivia, the chillies are commonly ground and dried before use, while in Peru, the pods are used fresh. The peppers are so tasty that they are often grilled, roasted or stuffed and eaten.

Growing Tips

As these chillies grow very tall and the fruits take such a long time to ripen, these are a little bit trickier to grow anywhere other than their native environment. They grow best under glass, in a position that gets full sun. This variety does well under grow lights in temperate climates.

For good germination, the soil temperature needs to remain above 18°C/65°F, and the plant is not tolerant of low temperatures. It is also very sensitive to water levels and too much water will kill a young plant.

Capsicum Pubescens

The *Pubescens* species is the least cultivated variety of chillies and is very different from the other varieties. They are easy to identify because they have hairy leaves and black seeds, and were named *Pubescens* from the Latin for hairy.

These chillies have a very distinct capsaicinoid content, which means they have a unique flavour and heat. Some members of this family are hot; hotter than the habanero. This species of chillies can withstand cooler temperatures than many of the other pepper plants.

This species is also native to Peru and Bolivia, though it has now spread throughout Latin America, but is rarely grown outside of this area. In Bolivia, these plants are known as 'locoto' whereas in Peru it is called 'rocoto.' The Mexicans refer to this pepper as 'manzano' which means apple, giving you an idea of the shape of the fruit.

Physical Characteristics
The leaves of this species are quite furry, which makes it very easy to identify this plant. The seeds are black, whereas all other chilli species have tan or lighter coloured seeds.

Pubescens flowers have petals which are typically a blue/violet colour, which is one of this species' distinctive features. The flowers usually grow in pairs or by themselves, though on rare occasions you will see clusters of four flowers.

The pods grow to the size of a small apple and mature to a red or yellow colour. The walls are surprisingly thick for their size and are very juicy and dense. As they mature, these chillies also develop a very peculiar yet strong pungent smell. The roots of this variety of chilli become woodier as the plant matures, and it is often called the 'tree chilli.'

Culinary Uses
Most of the other chilli species are processed in some way before use, often dried or crushed, whereas the *pubescens* varieties are usually eaten fresh as the pods are so dense and juicy. Because of this, these chillies are quite difficult to dry.

The smaller varieties are often used in fresh salsas, stuffed, deep fried, baked and served with fresh corn or sweet potatoes. Typically, these are stuffed with beef, pork or cheese which has been seasoned with spices such as garlic, onion or black pepper.

Growing Tips

What is particularly notable about the *pubescens* species is that it cannot cross-pollinate any of the other chilli varieties. Compared to other species, the pods of the *pubescens* family take longer to mature and grow to their full size.

Due to the long maturation time, seeds need to be sown either late winter or early spring to give the plant plenty of time to mature. Sow them in a sunny spot in a warm greenhouse or under lights. The seeds take three to four weeks to germinate and need to be kept at a consistent temperature of 20C/68F. When kept in a cool, damp environment and properly looked after, these plants will fruit for as many as fifteen years.

Popular Chilli Varieties

There are thousands of varieties of chilli, with new varieties being produced every year, particularly as breeders try to produce hotter and hotter chillies. Listing all of the chilli varieties would be excessive, so here are some of the most popular and commonly grown chilli varieties, including some we have already talked about. These are the varieties you are most likely to be able to order seeds for and those commonly talked about in chilli growing circles.

7-Pot Barrackapore Chilli

A member of the *chinense* family, this pepper is over one million on the Scoville scale. It originates from Trinidad and is quite rare, despite its heat level and unusual fruity taste. The pods have a similar shape to the habanero pepper, and the skin is usually pimpled. The immature pods are green and ripen to a bright red colour.

7-Pot Chilli

Another super-hot chilli, rating over a million on the Scoville scale. Heat wise, this is very similar to Bhut Jolokia, though it has a nuttier, fruitier flavour, which is common of the Caribbean peppers. Originating from Trinidad, the seeds are quite hard to find, and there are a few different varieties such as the Yellow 7-Pot, the Chocolate, and the 7-Pot Jonah. It is plumper than its relative, the Trinidad Scorpion Pepper, with a rough and pimpled skin. The name of this chilli refers to the fact it is hot enough to flavour seven pots of stew. In its home country, this pepper is so hot it is used in military grade tear gas and in a marine paint used to prevent barnacles sticking to surfaces.

African Bird's Eye/African Devil Chilli

Also known as Piri Piri or Pili Pili, this is a small chilli, growing to about an inch long. Rating 175,000 on the Scoville scale, it has a bit of a punch. Naturalised to Africa, it is now commercially grown and often used as an organic pest control. The mature fruits are purple or red, with a blunt tapered point. It is known in the West as providing the heat in Peri Peri sauce, though its flavour is not as interesting as other varieties.

Aji Amarillo Chilli
Popular in Peru and Chilli, this pepper is rarely grown outside of Latin America. It rates just 30,000 to 50,000 on the Scoville scale. Although it is not the hottest of chillies, it has a pleasant, fruity flavour that does not leave your mouth burning. It is named after the Spanish word for yellow, the fruits mature to a deep orange colour. If you visit a Latin American country, then you will find this chilli for sale and used in a lot of local cooking.

Aji Fantasy Chilli
A member of the *baccatum* family, this chilli was developed in Finland through five years of cross-breeding. It has a mild heat level but is very sweet and full of flavour. The plants are very productive, producing pods around the size of a habanero and, when ripe, are a lovely yellow colour.

Aji Limo Chilli
Another Peruvian chilli, this rates between 30,000 and 50,000 on the Scoville scale. Growing from two to three inches long, this variety comes in lots of different colours, from red to orange to yellow to white and even purple. It has a citrus/spice flavour and is commonly used in Peruvian cuisine.

Aji Panca Chilli
A mild chilli, rating just 500 on the Scoville scale, this pepper grows to three to five inches long, maturing to a burgundy/deep red colour. It is the second most commonly grown pepper in Peru, usually grown near the coast. It has a slightly smoky, sweet flavour, commonly used in Peruvian cooking.

Aji Pineapple Chilli
A member of the *baccatum* family, these peppers start off a green colour, maturing to vibrant yellow pods that are two or three inches long. It is moderately hot at 20,000 Scoville heat units and is rarely grown outside of Latin America.

Aleppo Chilli
Also known as the Halaby pepper, this member of the *annuum* family rates around 10,000 on the Scoville scale. It is named after a city in Northern Syria where it is often grown and used dried and crushed. Popular in Middle Eastern and Mediterranean cuisine, it has an aromatic, fruity flavour and is a lovely deep red colour. It makes for a great substitute for paprika, with a little bit more heat.

Anaheim Chilli

This a mild pepper, commonly grown in the USA where it is used in many different dishes. Growing to between six and ten inches long, it is often used while still green, but can be allowed to mature to a red colour where it is often dried into a ristra.

Anaheim chilli

Ancho Chilli

A mild chilli, rating just 1,000 to 2,000 on the Scoville scale, it is a dried poblano chilli with a sweet, moderate heat and a mild paprika-like flavour. When combined with the Pasilla and Mulato chillies, it forms the key component of the mole cooking sauces.

Bahamian Chilli

Originating from the Bahamas, hence the name, it is still a common commercial crop on the islands. This small, round pepper grows to just an inch in length but packs a significant punch, rating between 95,000 and 110,000 on the Scoville scale. The peppers of this plant grow upright in clusters rather than hanging down and come in a variety of colours from red to yellow to green and orange.

Banana Peppers

A very mild, sweet pepper also known as the yellow wax pepper. Rating no more than 500 on the Scoville scale, it is popular eaten raw, added to salads, on sandwiches or even adding to salsa. These peppers are usually used fresh and are picked when bright yellow in colour, though matures to orange or red.

Barker's Chilli

This chilli grows to between five and seven inches in length and rates between 15,000 and 30,000 on the Scoville scale. It is a variety of Anaheim pepper family and used in the same way as the Anaheim peppers. As the fruits mature into a deep red colour, so they grow hotter. With thin skins, they are ideal for roasting, stuffing, canning or giving a salsa a bit of a kick.

Bhut Jolokia Chilli / Ghost Pepper
This chilli is going to burn! Rating over a million on the Scoville scale, it is popular with chilli-heads purely for its heat. This a hybrid between *chinense* and *frutescens* peppers. In its home country, it is popular used to flavour fermented fish and pork.

Ghost pepper chillies

Bird's Eye Chilli

A very small chilli, common in Thailand, Vietnam, the Philippines and Cambodia, it rates between 50,000 and 100,000 on the Scoville heat scale. It is popular in Asian cuisine, though is now used across the world. They are very tiny and often used when pickling onions, gherkins or other vegetables to give the pickling mixture some kick. You can find these dried and in jars on the spice shelf in your local supermarket.

Bishop's Crown Chilli
A member of the *baccatum* family, this chilli has an unusual shape and is fruity yet spicy. Maturing to an inch long and two or three inches wide with a lovely red colour, this chilli can be anywhere between 5,000 and 30,000 Scoville. It is dried, pickled and commonly used in salsa dishes.

Bolivian Rainbow Chilli
This is a very pretty looking chilli plant with peppers that starts out bright purple, turning yellow, orange and then red as the pods mature. The nice thing about this plant is that peppers of all stage of maturity can be present at once, making it extremely colourful. Grown indoors, you will be harvesting

fruits throughout the year, though they need a warm climate if outdoors. These small peppers are cone shape and about an inch long, pack a bit of a punch, being between 10,000 and 30,000 on the Scoville heat scale.

Caribbean Red Chilli

A very hot pepper, originating from the Yucatan Peninsula in Mexico, rating between 300,000 and 475,000 on the Scoville scale. Now cultivated throughout the Caribbean and North America, this pepper is about an inch across and an inch and a half long. The bushes grow to about three feet tall and mature in approximately ninety days. This pepper is good to grow in cooler climates as it is well suited to container growing. It is a decorative plant, with delicious, fruity peppers that are popular in hot sauces and fiery salsas.

Carmen Italian Sweet Chilli

This pepper is shaped like a bull's horn and has a sweet, fruity taste. They are best when mature and a deep red colour. Ideal for cooler climates, these plants were specifically developed to fruit in cooler areas, though are not frost tolerant. The pods are tapered, usually about six inches long and two or three inches wide. This sweet pepper is popular when roasted and is common in many Italian dishes.

Carolina Cayenne Chillies

Similar in appearance to the cayenne chilli, this pepper is much hotter, ranking between 100,000 and 125,000 Scoville. It matures to a deep red colour and has thin, wrinkly skin. It is known to be resistant to root-knot nematode and is often used in crop rotation to reduce these harmful pests.

Carolina Reaper Chilli

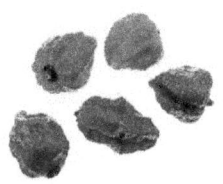

At the time of writing, this is the hottest chilli in the world, with a Scoville heat rating of 1,569,383 according to the Guinness Book of World Records. The peak heat level was measured at 2,200,000 Scovilles with the Smokin' Ed's Carolina Reaper ® variety. Bred by crossing a Pakistani Naga and a red habanero, this fruity pepper packs a serious punch and is positively dangerous. The plants grow to four feet tall, and the seeds are expensive but relatively easy to obtain.

Cascabel Chilli

An *annuum* chilli, this small chilli rates just 1,000 to 3,000 on the Scoville scale. It is also known as the ball chilli or Chile Bola in Spanish. Maturing to a deep red, it retains its colour when dried, taking on a brownish tint. This is great to use in soups, stews or salsas for providing a little heat without being too overpowering.

Cayenne Buist's Yellow Chilli
A very mild chilli, rating under 1,000 on the Scoville scale, this pepper is commonly used dried and crushed or added fresh to salsas.

Cayenne Chilli
A thin chilli, growing to two to three inches long, ranging from green to red in colour. Very commonly used in cooking, this chilli rates between 30,000 and 50,000 on the Scoville scale.

Cayenne chilli peppers

Charleston Hot Chilli
Very similar to the Carolina Cayenne, this chilli was created by the US Department of Agriculture. Rating 70,000 to 100,000 Scovilles, it is much hotter than the cayenne pepper. As the pods mature, they change colour from green to yellow to orange and finally a bright red colour. The pods are harvested at any stage of maturity, though are most commonly left to fully mature. The pods grow to about five inches long but just three-quarters of an inch wide.

Chilaca Chilli
A long, thin, curved chilli that reaches anywhere from six to nine inches in length but just an inch wide. Rating just 1,000 to 2,500 Scovilles, this pepper has a flat shape with wrinkled skin. It has a rich flavour when matured and an unusual deep, brown colour. Rarely used fresh, this chilli is most commonly used dried where it is known as Pasilla and used in sauces or ground into a condiment.

Chilli be Arbol Chilli

This thin, Mexican chilli can be anywhere from 15,000 to 65,000 on the Scoville scale, so be careful as you might get a surprise. It typically grows to between two and three inches long and is very thin, less than half an inch wide. They are harvested at full maturity, when they are red in colour. The chilli is a tree chilli as it has a very woody stem and is often called Bird's beak chilli or Rat's tail chilli. The dried chillies are commonly used in ristras or wreaths because they retain their colour well after drying.

Chilli Pequin Chilli

A member of the *annuum* family, this chilli, also known as the Bird Pepper, is reasonably hot, between 30,000 and 60,000 Scovilles. It grows wild in its native lands and is eaten and spread by wild birds. The fruit is extremely small, no more than three-quarters of an inch long. Immature pods are green, and as it matures, the fruits turn a bright red colour. It has an unusual flavour, a combination of nutty, smoky and citrus making it popular in a variety of dishes. It is made into hot sauces, soups, and used to give salsas a serious kick.

Chiltepin Chilli

A tiny, round chilli that is about half an inch or so in diameter yet rating between 50,000 and 100,000 Scovilles, so certainly not to be trifled with. It grows wild in the southern parts of Texas and northern Mexico. The mature pods are an orangey red to red colour.

Chimayo Chilli

Quite a cool chilli, rating only 4,000 to 6,000 Scovilles, it is another New Mexico chilli, but one that isn't grown commercially very often. It is more commonly grown at home and has a huge variety in shape and appearance, being anywhere from four to seven inches in length. It is rarely seen fresh outside of New Mexico, but can sometimes be found dried and powdered as Molido.

Chipotle Chilli

This is a smoked, dried jalapeño pepper with a Scoville rating of between 2,500 and 8,000. It has become very popular in American cuisine to provide heat and flavour, without being overpowering. Mature, red jalapeño peppers are harvested and smoked for several days until they are fully dried. Around ten pounds of jalapeño peppers will make a single pound of chipotle peppers.

Chocolate 7-Pot Chilli
This is a chilli that will blow your head off, rating somewhere between 923,000 and 1,850,000 Scovilles; it is to be handled with care. Originally from Trinidad, it is popular throughout the Caribbean. With a fruity, sweet and nutty flavour, it is great in many dishes, but the heat is intense and will make you sweat. This pepper is not grown commercially, though it is much sought after by chilli-heads for its heat and flavour.

Chocolate Habanero Chilli
Also known as Congo Black or Black Habanero, this is a hot pepper originally from the Caribbean. Ripening to a gorgeous chocolate brown, it is very hot, measured at between 300,000 and 425,000 Scoville heat units. It is a slow-growing plant with a long growing season, but well worth being patient for. The mature fruits are around three inches long and two inches wide with a rich, unique flavour. A little of this will go a long way, and it is popular in a lot of different dishes, including Jamaican Jerk Sauce.

Corno di Toro Giallo Chilli
A mild and sweet pepper, rating around 1,000 to 2,000 Scovilles. It is popular in a variety of dishes where it is used instead of the bell pepper for a bit of extra heat. This pepper is great grilled, roasted or eaten raw.

Coronado Chilli
A cool chilli, originating in South America with a Scoville rating of 700 to 2,000. The pods are about four inches long and two inches wide with a very thin, waxy skin. It turns bright red when mature and has a taste reminiscent of berries and pears. It is eaten fresh, ground and dried and added to many dishes for extra flavour.

Cubanelle Chilli
A sweet pepper with a little bit of heat, this chilli is under 1,000 Scoville. When ripe, the pods are a bright red colour, yet usually harvested when immature and a yellow/green colour. The banana-shaped fruits are between four and six inches long and around two inches wide, tapering to a blunt point at the bottom. Known as the Italian Frying Pepper, this chilli is, perhaps unsurprisingly, delicious fried in a little olive oil.

Datil Chilli
A chilli with intense heat, between 100,000 and 300,000 Scovilles, but with a much fruitier and sweeter flavour. The pods grow to around three inches in length and, when mature, are a yellow/orange colour. Most of the commercial supply of these chillies comes from a town in Florida called St. Augustine, which holds a Datil Pepper Festival every October.

Devil's Tongue Chilli
The heat of this pepper is quite intense, with a rating of between 125,000 and 325,000 Scovilles. When mature, it is a bright yellow or a yellow-orange colour with a fruity, sweet flavour.

Diablo Grande Chilli
The fruits of this variety start off yellow-green, maturing to a red colour with a narrow crescent shape to the pods. The fruits are relatively hot, between 60,000 and 100,000 on the Scoville scale. These chillies are used at any stage of maturity and are pickled, cooked or eaten fresh.

Dolmalik Chilli
This chill is very popular in Turkey, where it is used to season meats, is stuffed or even roasted. The peppers grow to about four inches long and around two inches wide with medium thick flesh. The plants themselves grow to about three feet tall, and the pods are a reddish brown colour when mature.

Dorset Naga Chilli
This is a very popular member of the *chinense* family, with a Scoville rating of between 1 and 1½ million, so certainly not for the faint of heart. It was developed in Dorset, England in 2001 by Joy and Michael Michaud. Bred from the Naga Monica chilli from Bangladesh, they bred the pepper over a number of years to end up with one of the fiercest on the market.

Doug des Landes Chilli
This is a sweet pepper variety that looks like a long Cayenne chilli that has been twisted. Originating in the south west of France in the Landes region, this chilli can grow to over a foot long with a sweet and fruity flavour. The peppers are used fresh or cooked and harvested anywhere from the immature green to the ripe red.

Dundicut Chilli
This member of the *annuum* family has a Scoville rating of between 55,000 and 65,000. The peppers are small and round, growing up to an inch in diameter. They are a dark red colour and popular in Indian and Pakistani cuisine. The flavour is similar to that of the Scotch Bonnet, but not quite as hot.

Elephant's Ear Chilli
Another member of the *annuum* family, this is a rare, sweet pepper of the paprika type developed in Croatia. As the pepper grows, it flattens and begins to resemble an elephant's ear. In its home country, it is roasted and stuffed

or used in a wide variety of sauces. The fully grown peppers are around six inches long and about four inches wide, ripening from green to red. The plant itself grows to around three feet tall.

Espanola Chilli
A fairly mild chilli, ranking just 1,500 to 2,000 on the Scoville scale, this was developed in New Mexico in the 1980's. The fruits grow up to seven inches in length, maturing from green to a deep red colour. The immature fruit are used to make chilli rellenos, and the mature fruit is often ground into a powder or used to make ristras. It is popular in cooking as it gives a dish a kick without being overwhelming.

Fatalii Chilli
Popular in central and southern parts of Africa, this chilli packs a punch, with a Scoville rating of between 125,000 and 325,000. It has the heat of the habanero chilli, but a fruity, citrus flavour. Unlike the habanero, whose heat kind of sneaks up on you, the Fatalii kicks you straight in the teeth, with an instant, very intense burn. The peppers grow to about three inches in length and mature to a nice yellow colour.

Fresno Chilli
This member of the *annuum* family has a Scoville rating of between 2,500 and 10,000. It is very similar in appearance to the jalapeño chilli, but can be much hotter. As they mature, they change colour from green to red, but they also increase in heat level, with the mature, red peppers being much hotter than the immature green ones. The green peppers tend to be a mild to medium hot, and this variety is often harvested and sold at this stage of development. The mature fruit is often much hotter than the jalapeño and grows to between two and three inches in length, with a diameter of around an inch. They are very common in the United States and are a popular chilli for salsa. These peppers do not dry very well and so are not used for chilli powder.

Frontera Sweet Peppers
This is a sweet pepper, below 1,000 Scoville units. The peppers are very similar to Scotch Bonnet, being round in shape and maturing to a bright yellow/orange colour. The fruits of this plant grow up three inches in diameter.

Gatherer's Gold Chilli
This is a horn-shaped chilli that ripped to a very attractive golden orange colour. This chilli has very thick walls and a delicious sweet flavour, with surprisingly few seeds. As an Italian sweet pepper, it is great for frying, roasting or eating raw.

Giant Szegedi Chilli
This sweet pepper was developed in Hungary and is heart shaped. It starts out as a yellow/white colour then, as it ripens, it turns orange and finally red when it is fully mature and has its sweetest taste. The fruit grows between four or five inches long, with plenty of flesh and thick walls. The plants are quite hardy for a chilli plant and prolific in their fruit production.

Spanish Naga Chilli
Also known as the Gibraltar Naga, this chilli rates an eye-watering 1,086,844 on the Scoville scale. It was developed in the United Kingdom from Indian chilli plants and is now frequently grown in Spain. The heat of these chillies is increased by growing them in a hot environment, which creates stress in the plant. The fruits grow up to three inches long with a tapered end. As they mature, the fruits change colour from green to red with a very wrinkled and knobbly skin.

Guajilli Chilli
This is a very popular chilli in Mexico and has mild or moderate heat, rating between 2,500 and 5,000 on the Scoville scale. When mature, the fruits are dark red, almost brown in colour with a leathery skin. The peppers are typically between three and five inches long and about an inch wide. The flavour is that of fruit or green tea, with a hint of berries. These chillies are usually sold whole and dried, then toasted and ground or made into a paste or sauce. In Mexico, you will often find this chilli sold as a ground powder.

Guntur Sannam Chilli
This is an Indian chilli, growing in the state of Andra Pradesh where it is a vital cash crop, and thousands of people depend on this chilli for their income. It rates between 35,000 and 40,000 on the Scoville scale and is used in cooking, as a vegetable or as a condiment.

Habanero Chilli
This is a very popular and well-known chilli named after the Cuban City, La Habana, also known as Havana. Rating anywhere from 80,000 to 600,000 on

the Scoville scale, this relative of the Scotch Bonnet was frequently traded in Cuba but is now grown in Mexico on the Yucatan Peninsula. It is also grown in the United States and other South American countries, notably Panama where it is called 'aji chombo'. This is one of the most familiar and popular peppers in use today.

Habanero Vanilla Chilli

Hatch Chilli
Grown in Hatch Valley, New Mexico, these chillies rate between 1,000 and 2,500 on the Scoville scale. The Hatch Valley is known as the chilli capital of the world as so many different types of chilli are grown there. This is a cultivar of the New Mexico green chilli, and there are many different varieties such as NuMex Big Jim, NuMex Heritage 6-4 and so on. Every year, the town of Hatch hosts a chilli festival on Labour Day which can attract up to 30,000 visitors into this tiny New Mexican town.

Hidalgo Chilli
Similar to the Serrano pepper and originating in Central America and Mexico, this chilli rates between 6,000 and 17,000 on the Scoville scale. The plant is quite prolific in its production of fruit, which grows up to two inches long with a shiny, thick red skin. This is a great pepper for pickling, though also used in salsa, sauces and as a relish due to the kick it gives the dishes.

HJ8 Total Eclipse Space Chilli
This is an interesting chilli, though not particularly hot with a Scoville rate of around 1,000. The seeds of this chilli were sent into space by China, exposed to cosmic radiation and zero gravity then returned to Earth where they are cultivated. The seeds are grown, and a small percentage show some form of mutation from their exposure to cosmic radiation. Some of these are bred and then sold as these varieties often have good disease resistance or have high yields.

Hungarian Wax Chilli
Bred in Hungary, this pepper can be confused with the milder banana pepper

but has more of a kick, rating between 5,000 and 15,000 on the Scoville scale. The fruit of this plant are normally harvested before maturity, while still yellow and around eight inches long and a couple of inches thick. When matured, the fruits grow larger and turn red, but then they are also much hotter.

Hungarian Wax Chilli

Infinity Chilli
Developed in the United Kingdom by Nick Woods, this held the world record for the hottest chilli for a short time in 2011, rating 1,176,182 on the Scoville scale. It has wrinkled skin, which is common in extremely hot chillies, and is very popular with chilli-heads for its heat. If you are growing this, be warned and wear gloves when handling any part of the plant.

Jalapeño Chilli
One of the best-known chilli peppers, this popular pepper only rates between 2,500 and 8,000 on the Scoville scale. Its mild to moderate heat is part of its popularity as it gives a good flavour without being overpowering. The fruits grow anywhere from two to six inches, though are known to grow longer. The fruits are usually used before they mature when they are still green, but when left to mature, the fruit turns red and is sweeter than the immature fruits. A typical plant will grow up to three feet in height, producing up to forty fruits. If you are growing this variety, regularly pick the fruit as it encourages the plant to produce even more chillies.

Jalora Chilli
This is a hybrid of the jalapeño developed by the Texas Agriculture Extension Service. It rates around 5,000 on the Scoville scale.

Jamaican Hot Chilli
Originating in Jamaica, there are a number of varieties of this pepper which typically rate from 100,000 to 200,000 on the Scoville scale. The Jamaican

Hot Chocolate chilli is brown with a ribbed and wrinkled skin, popular in marinades and hot sauces. The Jamaican Hot Red or Yellow Chilli is squash shaped and eaten fresh or pickled. These are popular in Caribbean cuisine and anywhere in the world where there is a Caribbean community, where you can sometimes find them in local shops.

Jwala Finger Hot Chilli
This chilli is one of the most popular in India, particularly the Gujarat region, giving spice and flavour to many Indian dishes. Rating between 20,000 and 30,000 on the Scoville scale, the name Jwala means volcano in Hindi. The fruits mature from green to red and are used dried or fresh. Growing to about four inches long, the fruits resemble a curved finger, having a wrinkled skin. The plants produce a good yield and are happy grown in the ground or in pots.

Lemon Drop Chilli
This chilli is bright yellow in colour and has a citrus taste about it, hence the name. Originating in Peru, where it is known as 'Kelli Uchu', it rates between 15,000 and 30,000 Scoville heat units. The fruits have a wrinkled skin and typically grow two or three inches long and about half an inch wide. If you like the taste of the habanero but are not so keen on the heat, then this is the perfect substitute chilli. Although the heat is still quite intense, it does not linger like the habanero, leaving behind a pleasant lemon flavour.

Liebesapfel Sweet Chilli
A very productive pepper with sweet, thick flesh. Its name means 'love apple' which gives you an idea of the shape of the fruit. It is a type of pimento pepper developed in Germany. The fruits are eye-catching, looking very much like tiny pumpkins and ripening from green through brown and finally to red. These are a very good pepper for stuffing.

Madame Jeanette Chilli
This chilli comes in a number of different forms with a Scoville heat rating of between 125,000 and 325,000. Its heat is similar to that of the habanero, though it has a very sweet flavour. Depending on the variety, the fruits will mature to a red or yellow colour. Originating in Suriname in South America, it is popular in local dishes.

Malagueta Chilli
This chilli looks very similar to the Bird's Eye chilli and has a Scoville rating of between 60,000 and 100,000. The fruit matures from green to red and grows to about two inches long. It is very popular in Brazil, but also commonly found in Mozambique and Portugal. It is named after a popular

West African spice but has no relation to it.

Mirasol Chilli
This chilli is one of the main ingredients in mole sauces and has a Scoville rating of 2,500 to 5,000. When dried, it is known as Guajillo, and the fruits are typically conical and up to five inches long. The mature fruit is a dark red, copper colour with a fruity, berry-like flavour. It is commonly used in Peruvian cuisine though is great in a wide variety of dishes with its distinct flavour.

Marita Chilli
These are smoked, mature (red) jalapeño peppers with a Scoville rating of between 2,500 to 10,000. These are smoked for less time than the chipotle pepper which means they are softer and fruitier in flavour.

Moshi Chilli
Originating from the village of Moshi in the foothills of Mount Kilimanjaro in Tanzania, Africa, this is a rare, but very hot chilli that has a high yield. The plants grow up to four feet high with the two-inch fruit ripening from green to red.

Mulato Chilli
This is a mild to medium dried Poblana pepper with a Scoville rating of between 2,500 and 3,000. This pepper ripens to a brown colour, and then dried. The mature fruit is around four inches long and two inches wide, tapering towards the end of the chilli. This, along with Ancho and Pasilla, is commonly used in the Mexican mole sauces. Its flavour is rather unique, with a chocolate or liquorice flavour with a hint of cherry. It is commonly ground into chilli powder and is great in many different dishes.

Naga Viper Chill
Another eye-watering chilli, this has a Scoville rating of 1,382,118. It is a hybrid of the Bhut Jolokia, Trinidad Scorpion and Naga Morich developed by Garland Fowler of the Chilli Pepper Company in Cumbria, England. Not commonly used in cooking due to its heat, this is mainly grown by chilli-heads and used in fiery hot sauces.

New Mex Big Jim Chilli
Developed in New Mexico in the 1970s, this chilli has a Scoville rating of between 2,500 and 3,000. The ripe fruits grow up to a foot long and mature to a lovely red colour. However, the fruits are more commonly harvested and used when immature and green in colour. This particular variety held the world record for the largest chilli ever grown. The flavour is mildly spicy and

it is popular in salads, salsas and chilli rellenos. The ripe fruits are often dried and made into ristras, but are great in almost any type of cuisine.

New Mexico 6-4 Heritage Chilli
Growing up to eight inches in length, this chilli has a great flavour and aroma, which develops even better when roasted. Developed in New Mexico, this chilli has a rating on the Scoville scale of 3,000 to 5,000.

New Mexico Scorpion Chilli
This super chilli has a Scoville rating of 1,191,595 and is popular with chilli-heads, often used in hot sauces.

Orange Thai Chilli
This is a thin chilli, similar in shape and size to the common red Thai chilli, though its pods are orange. They are medium hot, and the plants are quite productive, with a single plant producing as many as 200 peppers.

Paprika Chilli
A mild chilli, under 1,000 on the Scoville scale, this cone-shaped chilli is usually dried and ground to make the popular spice paprika. Originally developed in Hungary, this red pepper grows up to eight inches long.

Paprika Chilli

Pepperoncini Chilli
These sweet, Italian peppers are also known as Tuscan peppers or golden Greek peppers, with a Scoville rating of between 100 and 500. The thin peppers grow up to three inches in length with wrinkled skin, usually sold pickled. The skin starts off a yellow/green colour, turning red as the fruits mature. Although both colour fruits are found in stores, the green is the most commonly found. Fresh, these chillies are used in recipes such as pizza sauce.

Peter Pepper Chilli
This is a favourite chilli amongst many growers for its very distinctive phallic

shape, which gives it a number of nicknames, none of which are polite! With a Scoville rating of between 5,000 and 30,000, the fruits grow up to four inches long and about 1½ inches wide, maturing to a bright red colour. Originating in Louisiana and Texas, these are grown commercially, and seeds are available from suppliers. Although the chillies are typically grown for their novelty value, they are also great in a salsa.

Picuante/Peppadew Chilli
This is a popular pepper in South Africa, rating just under 1,200 Scoville heat units. It is particularly popular in its native country on pizza for its sweet taste and touch of heat. It looks very similar to a cherry tomato and is often stuffed or served with salads.

Pigment de Bresse Chilli
This is a rare, heirloom chilli grown in the Burgundy region of France. It is commonly ground into a powder and used in local cuisine, particularly in a cheese known as 'fromage fort.' The peppers ripen from green through to red with a sugary taste and rates somewhere between the jalapeño and cayenne chilli in heat level. The fruits grow to about five inches in length and approximately an inch wide.

Pimento Chilli
The pimento or pimiento chilli is also known as the cherry pepper, measuring between 100 and 500 on the Scoville scale. It grows up to four inches long with a width of around three inches. When mature, it is bright red and heart shaped. It is best known as it is used to stuff olives with.

Pimiento de Padron Chilli
This is a mild pepper, related to the previous one and grown in the Padron region of Spain. The fruits are small to medium in size, growing around three inches long, maturing from green through to a bright red colour. These are interesting as most of the chillies are very mild with virtually no heat, yet every now and then you will get one that has a bit of a kick to it.

Piquillo de Lodosa Chilli
Grown in the Basque and Navarre regions of Spain, this is a sweet pepper with very mild heat. They are often roasted, before being stored in oil or pickled, but is also great stuffed, roasted, fried or included in any number of sauces and dishes. The peppers grow to around two inches wide and ripen from green to red.

Poblano Chilli
A very well-known pepper, this has a Scoville rating of between 1,000 and

2,000. The fruits grow up to four inches long, starting out as a dark green colour, maturing to a brown or deep red. These are relatively large chillies, heart-shaped with thick walls, so they are ideal for stuffing. Poblano chillies are often dried and then referred to as ancho chillies. One of the most popular chillies in Puebla, Mexico, the plant only grows to about two feet tall, but the pods grow up to six inches in length and three inches wide.

Poblano Chilli

Purple Jalapeño Chilli
A smaller variety of the popular jalapeño chilli, this highly productive plant is often grown for ornamental purposes. With a heat rating of between 2,500 and 8,000, the immature peppers are green, maturing to a dark purple and finally a deep red colour. Often the plant will have fruits of all three colours on it at once, which makes it a great addition to any garden. Unlike some ornamental varieties, the fruits of this plant are edible and used in the same way as the jalapeño.

Purple Marconi Chilli
This is a very tasty Italian sweet pepper that grows to around six inches long. It has thin walls and can be red, purple or a golden colour. The bright red peppers are by far the sweetest, whereas the purple fruits have a more peppery flavour. The golden peppers are mild and sweet. The fruits are great for pretty much anything from eating raw to roasting and stuffing. The immature fruit is purple, and it ripens to a bright red colour, with fruit of all different colours on the plant at the same time.

Puya Chilli
This is a small, hot chilli with a Scoville rating of between 5,000 and 6,000, popular for its fruity flavour. Commonly used in sauces, it can be soaked in water and then the water used in cooking.

Red Amazon Chilli
This is a dried Tabasco chilli with a Scoville rating of 75,000. It is very commonly used in soups and sauces, or ground into a powder and used instead of cayenne pepper to give a dish more of a kick.

Red Sabina Habanero Chilli

This is a variety of the habanero chilli with a heat rating of between 200,000 and 580,000 Scoville. The fruit is bright red and is popular in hot sauces or used as a chilli powder, though it is also used in police grade pepper sprays.

Sandia Chilli

A New Mexico chilli with a Scoville rating of between 5,000 and 7,000. The peppers grow six or seven inches long and are very similar to the popular Anaheim pepper. The fruits ripen from green to red, though are often harvested when at the immature, green stage. These chillies are great for roasting, in salsas or for making chilli rellenos, though the red, ripe fruits are often used in ristras. This chilli is popular as it adds a kick to a dish without being overwhelming.

Santa Fe Grande Chilli

Commonly known as the yellow hot chilli, this fruit has a Scoville rating of just 500 to 700. The immature fruits start out a green/yellow colour, maturing through to orange to red and growing to about five inches long. The chillies are sweet and often served pickled.

Santana Chilli

This variety is popular in Japan and popular used in Asian cooking, particularly stir-fries. It has a Scoville rating of between 40,000 and 50,000. It is often ground into powder, used in sauces or salsas. The fruits are approximately two inches long, and the plant itself makes for an attractive ornamental addition to any garden. The fruits are cone-shaped and mature to a bright red colour with thin, wrinkled skin.

Scotch Bonnet Chilli

This cultivar of the habanero is very popular with home growers, with a Scoville rating of between 100,000 and 350,000. Although named after the traditional Scottish hat (the Tam o' Shanter), which it resembles, it is very popular in Caribbean cuisine. It is also used in Guyana and the Maldives, as well as some other countries. The fruits mature to a red or yellow colour and goes well with pork and chicken.

Senise Chilli

Known as Peperone Crusco when dried, this chilli is popular cultivar in Italy, in the area around the town of Senise. These horn-shaped peppers are used in local cuisine and usually picked when red. With thin walls and very little flesh, these are usually served fried and salted, though can be dried and used as a powder.

Serrano Chilli

This is a smaller version of the jalapeño, with a Scoville rating of between 5,000 and 23,000. The peppers grow up to four inches long and around half an inch wide. They have plenty of flesh and so aren't particularly good for drying. They are most commonly found when green, though can be anything from yellow through to orange and red.

Serrano Chilli

Shepherd's Ramshorn Chilli

This is a large, sweet pepper that was developed in Spain, but is now very popular in Italy. It is a good pepper to grow in cooler, wetter areas as it has a relatively short growing season. It is usually eaten raw, roasted or stuffed.

Shipkas Chilli

This chilli has a striking resemblance to a carrot, being long, narrow and bright orange. With a heat rating of 5,000 to 30,000 Scovilles, it has a hot but fruity flavour. The fruits grow up to four inches long, and the plant was developed in Bulgaria. It is great roasted but also good in chutneys, marinades, and salsas.

Sonora Chilli

A mild Anaheim pepper that grows up to ten inches long and an inch and a half wide. With a Scoville rating of between 300 and 600, the fruits are commonly used in their immature, green form, though mature to a red colour. With thick, sturdy skin, these chillies are great for rellenos and have a good level of disease resistance. These are popular in the northwest of the United States where they are dried, pickled or used in salads or salsas.

Sucette de Provence Chilli
This is an heirloom chilli, developed in the Provence region of France. The fruits are long and thin, growing up to six inches long and just half an inch wide. The immature fruits are green, and they ripen through orange to a brilliant red colour. The heat level varies significantly, from mild to quite hot, similar in heat to a Serrano pepper. Their fruity flavour makes them very popular in French cooking where they are often roasted whole.

Sugar Rush Chilli
This is a rare, sweet chilli that originates in Peru. Its heat level is similar to a habanero, but not quite as hot. The fruits are peach coloured, which is extremely unusual in chillies. The plants grow to over five feet in height and need staking to prevent damage to the bush.

Super Chilli Chilli
This small pepper matures from green through orange to red and have a heat rating of between 40,000 and 50,000 Scovilles. Thriving in a hot and humid environment, the cone-shaped fruits will grow up to two inches long and an inch wide. These are very decorative, often used as ornamental plants in a garden. It is commonly used in Thai and Szechwan cuisine.

Sweet Apple Chilli
This is a very sweet chilli with a Scoville rating of 1,000 or so. It is often used instead of bell peppers to make a dish more interesting. It has a fruity flavour and a little bit of heat making it ideal for stuffing or using in soups, stews or sauces.

Sweet Bell Peppers
This member of the chilli family is probably the one you are most familiar with. These have no heat at all and are very mild. They are typically available in colours from green to orange, yellow and red, depending on the plant and maturity of the fruit.

Bell Peppers

Tabasco Chilli
This is the chilli used to make the famous hot sauce, with a heat rating of 30,000 to 50,000. It is a member of the *frutescens* family. The fruit is no more than two inches long, starting out a creamy yellow colour and maturing through orange to bright red. It is named after a state in Mexico where it is still grown today. Tabasco sauce is made in a place called Avery Island in Louisiana where they grow the peppers used in their famous sauce which has been made there since 1868.

Tabiche Chilli
This chilli was originally developed in India, though is now grown across the world where it prefers a hot, dry growing environment. Measuring between 85,000 and 115,000 on the Scoville scale, this is a hot chilli, shaped like a teardrop. It grows up to three inches long and about an inch wide with thin, wrinkled skin, maturing to a glossy red or pale yellow.

Tangerine Dream Chilli
This is a rocket-shaped sweet pepper that matures to a bright orange colour, hence its name. It has barely any heat, with the main focus being on sweetness. The plants themselves are small, only growing to about 18 inches tall, with upright peppers about three inches in length. These peppers are great in salads, pickled or roasted.

Thai Chilli
There isn't a single Thai chilli plant, but instead, this seems to account for many different species, all of a very similar size and shape. The Thai chilli is very small but very strong, with a Scoville rating of between 50,000 and 100,000. These chillies are popular in Thai cuisine and grown in Thailand, hence the name.

Tien Tsin Chilli
This chilli originates in China and has a Scoville rating of between 50,000 and 75,000. It is popular in many cuisines, notable Asian such as Szechwan and Hunan and is usually a couple of inches long and bright red. It is a key ingredient in the popular Kung Pao chicken dish.

Tiger Paw NR Chilli
Developed in Charleston, South Carolina, this is a very hot chilli from the habanero family. With a Scoville rating of between 265,000 and 328,000, it certainly packs a punch, but interestingly, was not developed for its heat but its resistance to root-knot nematodes, hence the NR in the name.

Trinidad Moruga Scorpion Chilli

This is an incredibly hot chilli, with a Scoville rating of 2,009,231, and yes, you have read that correctly. Indigenous to the Moruga region of Trinidad and Tobago, this is not a chilli to be messed with. It is generally used in super-hot sauces rather than day to day cooking.

Trinidad Perfume Chilli

This is a very mild chilli, rating under 500 on the Scoville scale. The fruits are small, about an inch and a half long and almost the same width. They mature from green to a bright yellow colour and give off a perfumed scent when cooked. They have a citrus taste, similar to the habanero chilli, but with a smoky edge to it.

Trinidad Scorpion Butch T Chilli

Another super-hot chilli variety rated at 1,463,700 on the Scoville scale.

Trinidad Scorpion Chilli

These chillies are shaped like a scorpion, though are red and wrinkly. They measure over 300,000 on the Scoville scale, so are not to be messed with. This plant takes around eighty days to mature and are great to grow indoors or in containers. The fruits mature from green to a very vibrant red. These are commonly used in marinades, salsas and hot sauces.

Tshololo Chilli

This is quite a rare chilli, originating in Brazil and rating between 80,000 and 120,000 on the Scoville scale. The fruit grows to about five inches in length and curls up similarly to the cayenne pepper.

Yatsafusa Chilli

This chilli is popular in Japan and is a small plant with yellow flowers. The chillies, rating around 75,000 Scovilles, grow upward and mature to about three inches long and a deep red colour. The peppers are often picked when still green for a milder flavour. You can find immature and mature peppers mixed in a dish to give the best flavour.

Popular Chillies by Heat Level

There are a lot of chillies available, literally thousands of different species. Here are some of the most commonly grown varieties listed by heat level to help you identify the right chilli to grow at home. Remember that the immature fruits tend to be milder than the mature ones so feel free to harvest the chillies before they mature if you want to keep the heat levels right down.

Mild Chillies
Not everyone wants to grow gut-burning chillies. Some people quite like the flavour, but may not be so keen on the heat. There are a lot of different mild chillies available, with these being some of the best to grow at home:

- Fresno Supreme – a mild chilli with thick flesh that is great in stir-fries
- Pasilla Basil – a fruity flavour
- Padron – the Spanish tapas pepper, commonly used when small and green
- Hungarian Black – great flavour from small, brown to black fruits

Medium Chillies
These are some popular medium-hot chillies that you could try growing:

- Georgia Flame – nice, thick flesh and a sweet yet spicy flavour
- Krimson Lee – also has thick, sweet flesh and is very good on a pizza
- Portugal – a large cayenne style fruit that is medium hot
- Rococo Red – quite slow to mature and looks like a miniature bell pepper
- Joes Long Cayenne – dries well and makes great paprika

Hot Chillies
Although these may not be the hottest chillies in the world, they will make your eyes water and are popular amongst growers. These are the hardest to grow and require very specific germination conditions, but you will be rewarded with some super-hot chillies.

- Friars Hat – brightly coloured fruits that are short and squat
- Ring of Fire – very hot peppers that are good for drying, similar in appearance to cayenne
- Carolina Reaper – the world record holder at the time of writing, a

searingly hot chilli that you will regret in the morning
- Pusa Jwala – a knobbly chilli that is very popular in Indian curries
- Trinidad Scorpion – resembles the curl of a scorpion's tail and extremely hot
- Chocolate Bhut Jolokia – extremely hot chilli that should be handled with care

The Scoville Scale Explained

The Scoville Scale is used to measure the heat of chillies. It is a measure of the capsaicin found in the fruits that gives them the burning heat they are known for. Capsaicin stimulates the chemoreceptor nerve endings, particularly in the mucous membranes of your nose and mouth. The higher the Scoville rating, the greater the amount of capsaicin present and the hotter the chilli. Often these are abbreviated to SHU or Scoville Heat Units.

In 1912, Wilbur Scoville, an American Chemist working for the Parke Davis Pharmaceutical Company, created a test which rated the pungency or heat levels of chilli peppers. This is known as the Scoville Organoleptic Test, and the result is often such referred to as a measurement in Scovilles.

An extract of the chilli is diluted in sugar syrup, which is presented to a panel of tasters, typically five people, until the heat of the extract can no longer be tasted by the testers. How much the solution has had to be diluted to get to this stage determines where the chilli rates on the Scoville scale. A bell pepper, which is sweet, has no heat and so rates zero. However, a pepper such as the bhut jolokias has a Scoville rating of about a million, meaning it has to be diluted a million times before the capsaicin in the chilli can no longer be tasted.

One disadvantage of this test is that it is subjective. One taster may be more sensitive to capsaicin than another, so the results were not always accurate. Although Scoville attempted to find other, more accurate tests, he never managed to find a better way of measuring the heat in chilli peppers.

In the 1970's, a new method of testing the heat levels was developed by a chemist called Gillett using High-Performance Liquid Chromatography or

HLPC. This directly measures the capsaicinoid level and relates it to the Scoville scale using a mathematical conversion.

Again, because of the conversion from ASTA pungency units from this test to the internationally recognized Scoville scale, the results are typically between 20% and 40% lower than the original test would have provided.

The Scoville scale ratings should not be taken as an absolute guide to the heat of a chilli pepper as there are many influencing factors in the heat level. The climate, humidity, soil, watering levels, amount of light received, and other environmental factors influence the heat level as does the genetic lineage of the seed itself. A chilli could have a heat rating of over a million when grown in an ideal climate such as New Mexico, yet when grown somewhere cooler and damper, such as in New England, may struggle to reach 300,000 Scovilles. However, not all fruits from a single plant will have the same heat rating; some will be hotter than others, so be warned, you may find an unusually hot chilli on your plant.

The level of heat of a chilli is very subjective. Some people have a greater tolerance for the heat of chillies, so a chilli which might make my eyes water may not make you blink. I would recommend trying something like a jalapeño, scotch bonnet or Tabasco sauce to determine your tolerance for chilli heat. Local ethnic stores often have quite a range of peppers, though sometimes they can be hard to properly identify, so be careful. This should give you a good idea of what types of chillies to grow based on their Scoville rating. Over time, you will get used to the hotter chillies, but starting out too hot can make you quite unwell.

Here are some of popular chillies and their Scoville ratings. You can buy seeds for most of these online and grow them at home. Bear in mind that the hotter the chilli, the harder it is to grow and the more careful you will have to be to create the ideal growing environment. As a comparison, some of the cooler chillies are included in this table to give you an idea of just how hot some of these chillies are.

Type of Chilli Pepper	Scoville Rating
Pure capsaicin	16,000,000
Police grade pepper spray (USA)	2,500,000 – 5,300,000
Carolina reaper	1,000,000 – 2,200,000

Trinidad moruga scorpion	1,000,000 – 2,000,000
Bhut jolokia (ghost pepper)	855,000 – 1,041,472
Red Sabina habanero	350,000 – 580,000
Habanero / Scotch bonnet	100,000 – 350,000
Tabasco chilli	30,000 – 50,000
Serrano chilli	6,000 – 23,000
Chipotle / jalapeño chilli	3,500 – 10,000
Paprika / pimento	100 - 900

As you can see, some of the chillies in everyday use are very much milder than the super-hot varieties. You are unlikely to find anything hotter than a Scotch bonnet in a regular shop, and even then you may struggle. However, Asian, African or South American retailers or markets are the best places to find the super-hot chillies, as the locals will buy them from these shops for use in their cooking at home. There is a predominantly Asian Indian area near to where I live, and they have several different fruit and vegetable stores. They are a great place to find unusual chillies, many of which are on the hotter end of the scale.

What Is Capsaicin?

The active component of chillies that makes your mouth burn is Capsaicin (8-methyl-N-vanillyl-6-nonenamide). It is a chemical irritant that affects mammals and creates a burning sensation in any tissue it comes into contact with. Capsaicin and some related alkaloids are collective known as capsaicinoids and were developed by the plants as a deterrent against being eaten. Pure capsaicin is colourless, very pungent, hydrophobic and a waxy/crystalline sold.

The placental tissue, that ribs and internal membranes that hold the seeds, is the main place capsaicin is found. However, the flesh parts of these fruits also contain some capsaicin. How much it contains depends on the cultivar with some containing far more than others. The seeds themselves contain no capsaicin and the highest concentration is found in the white pith on the inner wall of the chilli where the seeds are attached.

In the wild, chilli plants rely on birds to propagate the seeds. Birds are not affected by the burning sensation that affects humans and other mammals so the seeds can pass through their digestive tract to germinate later. Mammals have molar teeth that crush the seeds so they cannot germinate. Over a long period of time, natural selection led to some varieties increasing capsaicin production to prevent the seed pods being eaten by animals that do not disperse the seeds and help the plant reproduce.

There is some evidence that the purpose of capsaicin may also be as an anti-fungal component. *Fusarium*, a fungal pathogen, infects wild chillies and reduces the viability of seeds. Capsaicin acts as a deterrent to this pathogen, helping the plant to spread its seeds.

Capsaicin causes a burning sensation when it comes into contact with mucous membranes, so is often used in food products to add some piquancy, or heat. The most commonly used spices are paprika, a type of chilli, and a generic chilli powder. The level of heat, as you know from the previous section, is measured on the Scoville scale and some people love it whereas it really doesn't agree with other people.

Weirdly, people experience pleasure and even a euphoric effect when they eat capsaicin. The chilli-heads claim this is because the pain from the burning sensation releases endorphins.

As well as providing flavour to food and entertainment when watching people try to eat hot chillies, capsaicin also has medicinal uses. In concentrations of between 0.025% and 0.1%, it is used topically in dermal patches and ointments to provide pain relief. It is applied topically to relieve muscle and joint aches and pains such as those that come with arthritis, strains, sprains and general backache.

It can also reduce the symptoms of peripheral neuropathy, such as the post-herpetic neuralgia that you get after you have had shingles. Further studies have shown that a high (8%) dose of capsaicin topically provided 'moderate to substantial pain relief' from HIV-neuropathy, diabetic neuropathy and post-herpetic neuralgia. While capsaicin creams are used to reduce itching from psoriasis, clinical trials have not shown enough evidence of a positive effect. Researchers have also shown that capsaicin moderately decreases LDL cholesterol levels.

You have probably heard of pepper spray, but possibly hadn't made the connection between it and chillies. Capsaicinoids are an active ingredient in pepper sprays, which cause pain and breathing difficulty when it comes in contact with skin, eyes or mucous membranes.

Capsaicin is also great at deterring pests, particularly mammals such as deer, squirrels, bears, voles and dogs. It can also be used as an insect repellent and a spray of chilli and garlic is an effective treatment against aphids. Ground or dried chilli pods can be added to birdseed to keep rodents, particularly squirrels away from it. The chillies have no effect on the birds, but the squirrels will stay away. In Africa, chillies are a sustainable crop to keep elephants away from crops, which, fortunately, isn't a problem most of us will have.

As you know, capsaicin is a very strong irritant and needs proper handling such as protective goggles and gloves. When dealing with pure capsaicin, respirators and hazardous material handling procedures are required as it effects the skin immediately upon contact.

One of the most common plant related causes of admissions to poison centres is exposure to capsaicin. Hot chillies can cause burning pain to the skin and, when eaten, can produce abdominal pain, burning diarrhoea, vomiting and nausea. Anyone who has eaten a dish with hot chillies in will attest to this. In children, even a small amount of capsaicin can cause these effects. If you get capsaicin in your eyes, then you will feel extreme pain and your eyes will tear. Even getting capsaicin in your nose by scratching your nose while preparing chillies will make your eyes water and hurt. Don't even think about touching your genital region after preparing chillies as it is something you will regret for several days.

If you get capsaicin on your skin, then bath the affected areas with oily compounds such as paraffin oil, Vaseline or petroleum jelly or even vegetable oil. Polyethylene glycol is the most effective way to treat this pain as it removes any capsaicin that hasn't been absorbed by the skin. Soap or any detergent can be used to wash capsaicin off the skin, but plain water will have no effect. As capsaicin is soluble in alcohol, this is another way to clean contaminated items.

When you ingest capsaicin, the best treatment is to drink cold milk. The caseins (protein) in milk has a detergent effect on capsaicin and stops the burning sensation. A 10% sugar solution at 20°C/68°F has a very similar effect. If you do not take anything at all, the burning sensation will fade away after several hours.

Capsaicin is a member of the vanilloid family and binds to the TRPV1 receptor (vanilloid receptor subtype 1). TRPV1 is an ion channel type receptor that can be stimulated by protons, physical abrasion and heat. When activated, it allows cations to pass through the cell membrane. This depolarises the neuron and stimulated it to send a signal to the brain. The capsaicin molecule binds to the TRPV1 receptor and produces a sensation very similar to too much heat or even abrasive damage. This is why the spiciness of a chilli is described as a burning sensation while not causing any direct tissue damage.

Health Benefits of Chillies

Although fiery hot, and enjoyed by plenty of people for that, chillies are very beneficial for your health. Obviously, you shouldn't eat the super-hot chillies if you cannot tolerate them, but eat chillies that you can tolerate and enjoy. There are plenty of mild chillies that are full of flavour without having lots of spice. My elderly Italian neighbour swears that his long life and good health (he is in his 80's and still gets up ladders to repair his house) is down to eating some chillies every meal. He grows plenty of chillies every year and regularly tells me how good they are for my health.

Chillies are a member of the *Solanaceae* or nightshade family, like tomatoes, potatoes, and aubergines in the genus *Capsicum*. There are thousands of chilli cultivars grown all over the world, with certain varieties being more popular in certain areas. Some, such as the jalapeño and Tabasco pepper, are popular all over the world, whereas others have appeal to a more limited geographical area or specific ethnic group. Many varieties of chillies have been adopted by different ethnic groups and naturalised in their local area, such as the piri-piri pepper from Africa and the many chillies that have made their home in Indian cuisine. In India, different regions have different specialist chillies and the local markets are full of brightly colour chillies for sale.

The humble chilli has a wide variety of uses in improving your health, many of which come from the alkaloid compound, capsaicin. This is the same compound which gives chillies their kick and has had a great deal of investigation into its health benefits.

Scientific studies show that capsaicin has a wide variety of beneficial properties including being anti-carcinogenic, anti-bacterial, anti-diabetic, analgesic and even having the ability to reduce LDL cholesterol. Of course, pharmaceutical companies are working to take these benefits and put them into a capsule to sell you, but you can grow chillies at home for a few dollars and get many of the same benefits plus you get to enjoy the flavour of the chillies themselves.

As well as this, fresh chillies, particularly red and green ones, have very high levels of vitamin C. A 100g/4oz portion of fresh chillies contains around 240% of the recommended daily allowance of vitamin C. This vital vitamin is a very powerful antioxidant that is essential for collagen synthesis in your body. Collagen is essential for healthy bones, skin, and organs. Vitamin C has many other benefits to your body and is known to help strengthen the immune system and fight infection, particularly when taken with zinc and vitamin B12.

Chillies also contain other valuable antioxidants including vitamin A, beta-carotene, and lutein, amongst others. Again, these are important in fighting free radicals and maintaining a healthy immune system,

The benefits of chillies don't stop there; they are also high in essential minerals such as iron, magnesium, potassium, and manganese. All of these are essential for a healthy body and often missing from the modern Western diet.

B-complex vitamins are very important for the healthy function of the human body, and vegetarians, in particular, miss out on B vitamins as they are most commonly obtained from meat. Chillies are high in niacin, vitamin B6, vitamin B1 and thiamin.

A 100g/4oz portion of fresh chillies will give you a very high dose of essential vitamins and minerals. To give you an idea, this is what you would get, shown as a percentage of the recommended daily allowance:

- 240% vitamin C
- 39% vitamin B-6
- 32% vitamin A
- 13% iron
- 14% copper
- 7% potassium

Of course, these figures are a rough guide as the exact quantities will vary according to the growing environment and chilli cultivar. Factors such as soil quality, nutrient levels, and even the level of sunshine can influence the vitamin levels.

Chapter 2

How to Grow Chilies at Home

Growing chilli plants at home can be tricky, and this chapter is all about how you can successfully grow these often difficult plants at home. Once you understand the needs of the chilli plant, they are not too difficult to grow, but it is important you recognise the growing conditions each variety requires in order for them to produce fruit and mature. If you give them the right conditions, then they are much more likely to reward you with fruit. Most chilli growing problems stem from them not having the right germination or growing conditions.

Before You Start Growing Chillies

You need to be prepared to grow chillies as this avoids a lot of the common problems and issues. This book is one of the main things you need before you start, which teaches you everything you need to know to grow chillies successfully. You will also need other equipment. What you need depends a lot on where in the world you are. As we progress through this section, I will talk about what you need to grow chillies successfully in different climates.

Chillies are harder to grow in cooler climates and need more equipment to produce a successful harvest. In a hot climate, chillies are much easier to grow because you can grow them outside. In cooler climates, they need more care and attention, but you can still grow them successfully, so don't worry about how far north you are.

Equipment Needed

To grow chillies, you need some equipment. The basic equipment needed is the same no matter where in the world you are. Then in the cooler climates, you need some additional equipment to successfully germinate and grow chillies.

- Starter Pots – you need some pots to start your chillies off in. I would recommend small, three to five-inch plastic pots. I do not recommend peat pots or the cardboard from the inside of toilet rolls as these have a habit of getting too damp and growing mould or drying out too quickly and stressing the seedling. Ensure there are suitable drainage holes in the bottom of the pots you decide to use.
- Potting Compost – buy a good quality potting compost that is peat free, which makes it more environmentally friendly. Look for one

that is specifically designed for seeds. Avoid cheap compost as it tends to contain a lot of lumps which will prevent your plants from growing well and may also be low in nutrients. Also, avoid those containing miracle-gro or other additives as these are not always good for the plant and often kills beneficial micro-organisms in the soil.

- Vermiculite – this retains moisture, which helps prevent the soil from drying out. Add this to the potting compost and sprinkle some on top of the soil after placing the seed on the soil.
- Larger Pots – your chillies need potting on as they grow, so you will need nine or ten-inch pots to transplant the chillies into once they are ready.
- Plant Food – a good quality plant food is required; we'll discuss this in more detail later on.

In colder climates, some additional equipment will come in very helpful to help germination and keep the plants healthy. Unfortunately, in colder climates, the growing season is shorter, which means that chillies do not have enough time to mature fully when grown outside so need to be, at the very least, started off early in the season indoors. The following equipment will ensure the seeds germinate successfully and grow to maturity.

- Heated Propagator – chillies, particularly the hotter ones, require a certain level of heat to germinate correctly. A heated propagator provides this and ensures a high level of germination. Just make sure you keep the seeds moist enough as the soil can dry out with the heat.
- Grow Lights – if you are growing indoors, then grow lights give the plants the light they need, and some bulbs will also provide heat too. Depending on the bulbs you are using, you may need to change them during the fruiting phase to give your plants the right spectrum of light. Remember to keep the lights far enough away from the plants to prevent the heat from burning the leaves. You have to keep moving the lights up as the plants grow taller to prevent this. It is often worth pinching the tops off chilli plants when grown under lights so that they do not grow into the lights and become bushier.
- Greenhouse/Polytunnel – useful for growing your chillies outside and extending the growing season so that the plants can mature and fruit.
- Larger Pots – helpful for the mature plants to ensure that they have enough room to grow a strong root system to support the plants.

Although this is the basic equipment, there are many other items you could buy such as moisture meters, pH meters and more, but this is all you need to get started and to successfully grow chillies at home.

Where to Buy Seeds

Chilli seeds can be bought from almost any seed supplier and many shops. Most of these will stock the popular varieties of chilli such as jalapeño, scotch bonnet or generic chilli seeds. They will usually stock one or two sweet or bell pepper varieties.

For the more specialist peppers such as Hungarian hot wax, Carolina Reaper, and Habanero, you may need to go to a specialist supplier, typically online, though as chillies have grown in popularity, unusual varieties are finding their way into mainstream supplier catalogues. I would recommend avoiding 'cheap' suppliers on sites such as eBay as you may not get the seeds you think you are getting. Always use a reputable supplier as you know you are going to get what you wanted and they will germinate into the plants you are expecting.

For the rarer chillies, you are going to have to hunt around and find specialist growers or suppliers, which may not be local. There are some growers who specialise in growing chillies and sell rare chilli seeds, though be aware that rare seeds can be expensive.

If you are ordering chilli seeds from a different country, make sure you are aware of import laws. Depending on where you are in the world, you may not be able to import the chilli seeds from abroad. Some countries will not allow seeds to be imported due to the risk of contamination and introducing diseases or pests. If you are visiting a foreign country and bringing seeds back, make sure you check with customs as you could get into a lot of trouble illegally importing seeds and receive a heavy fine.

Can I Grow Chillies Where I Live?

You can grow chillies anywhere in the world. In hotter areas, you can grow them outside but in cooler areas, the growing season is too short for the plants to mature before the first frosts kill these tender plants off. Check the minimum temperatures in your area and the requirements of the type of chilli you are growing. Depending on where you are, you may have to start your chillies indoors and then plant outside or keep them in a greenhouse.

In cooler areas, chillies need to be grown either indoors or under glass because the growing season is not long enough for them to mature outside.

I'd recommend growing them in containers in a greenhouse or polytunnel if you don't want to grow them in your house.

In cooler climates, chillies are treated as annuals and will die back in the cold. Moving them indoors or into a greenhouse can allow them to survive the winter providing the ambient temperature doesn't drop too low. In hotter climates, chillies will grow outside and are treated as perennials.

Chillies can be grown anywhere in the world; you need to take into account the climate and adjust your growing techniques appropriately.

Growing Indoors vs. Outdoors

In cooler climates, you are not going to be able to grow chillies outdoors. You can grow them in containers and move them outdoors during hot spells, but the risk of later or early frosts means they cannot be grown outside all of the time. Mine are usually grown in a greenhouse, but during hot spells, they are moved outside so they can enjoy the heat and air circulation.

Chillies will thrive when grown indoors providing they get sufficient light and have a big enough container. One or two plants can be grown on a sunny windowsill, though you may want to choose smaller, bush type chilli plants and control their size, so they don't grow too big and take over.

Growing more or bigger plants indoors requires more specialist growing equipment. You can grow them in a hydroponic environment, where they do very well indeed or in soil under grow lamps.

The downside to growing indoors is the space that chilli plants take up, which is why many people use greenhouses or polytunnels. The advantage of these is that they extend the growing season enough so that the chilli plants can fully mature. In colder areas, they will not protect the plants from the cold of winter unless they are heated. You can learn everything you need to know about growing in a greenhouse in my book, Greenhouse Gardening, available on Amazon and in all good bookstores. This explains everything from choosing a greenhouse to building one and successful growing plants, including chillies.

Tips for Growing Chillies in Cooler Climates

When growing in a cooler environment, there are some steps you can take to improve germination rates and ensure a successful harvest of chillies. These are particularly important when you are growing the hotter varieties as these are much more sensitive and harder to grow. Even sweet peppers need special treatment in cooler environments.

To help germination, fill a multi-cell seed tray with a good quality seed compost. Put a single seed in each cell, then cover with a thin layer of vermiculite.

Using a fine rose watering can, water the seeds gently, cover with plastic wrap and put somewhere warm. Keep an eye on them, ensuring the compost remains moist but not wet. Within two to four weeks, you should see some growth at which point, move them to a warm spot with plenty of light but out of direct sunlight and remove the plastic wrap. Watering from below will encourage your seedlings to develop a strong root system. Capillary matting is excellent for this, but check every day that the soil surface is moist.

When the seedlings develop a second set of leaves, transplant them to 3"/7cm pots with a good quality compost in. Feed once a week with a liquid tomato feed.

As soon as the plants are five or six inches (12-15cm) tall, move the plants again to a 5"/12cm pot. When they reach eight inches tall, push a cane into the pot and carefully tie the plant to the cane to support it.

When the plants reach 12"/30cm tall, pinch out the top of the plant, typically above the fifth set of leaves. This encourages the plant to grow bushier so it produces more fruit. Re-pot again if required and check every day for aphids, which can quickly overwhelm a plant.

Flowers will appear and, unless you are putting your plants outside during the day, you need to pollinate the flowers by hand. Gently press a cotton bud into the middle of each flower, which pollinates them. In a greenhouse, leave windows open to encourage pollinators in, but when growing indoors, hand pollination is the only method.

As the first chillies appear, cut them off while they are green to encourage the plant to produce more fruit. Allow the next set of fruit to fully mature if you want.

In areas such as the United Kingdom, chillies are typically planted in January or February, though in warmer areas you can plant as late as May. This gives the plants plenty of time to mature, and you can plant them outside if the weather is warm enough where you live.

The hotter chilli cultivars have a longer growing season than cooler varieties. The hotter the growing environment, the hotter the chillies will be.

If you can overwinter your chilli plants, then they will produce higher yields in subsequent years and produce fruit earlier. Most chilli plants will be productive for up to five years, and after that, the yields fall.

Chillies grow well in cooler environments, and many people in more northerly latitudes can successfully grow chillies. So even if you don't live in a hot climate, you can still grow chillies and enjoy a great harvest, you just need to protect the plants from the weather.

How to Grow Chilli Plants

Chilli plants are notoriously tricky to grow; some varieties are relatively easy whereas others, usually the hotter and more exotic cultivars, can be extremely hard to germinate. It is important that you give the plants a lot of care, particularly while they are young. Most varieties have a long growing season and are extremely sensitive to fluctuations in temperature.

However, with a little bit of care and attention, it is possible to grow chillies successfully. This section is a complete guide to growing chillies, starting from seed. Remember you can buy plug plants which are pre-grown chilli seedlings, though you will be very limited in the varieties that you can buy unless you find a specialist plant nursery.

The hotter chilli varieties are the hardest to germinate and grow, being much more sensitive to environmental conditions than milder varieties. Seedlings like constant heat to germinate reliably and prefer hotter temperatures. To grow very hot chillies, the plants need to be kept in a hot environment. Pay attention to the growing environment and provide them with the right conditions and your chillies will do very well indeed.

Sowing & Germinating Your Seeds

Once you have sourced your seeds, the next step is to germinate them. This is where most people struggle and the first obstacle for you to overcome. You can use multi-cell seed trays or small, single pots. I'd avoid the large, open planting trays purely because the roots can get entangled. In these trays, it's very easy to damage a seedling trying to re-pot it as the seedlings are very delicate and easy to damage.

Use a good quality, store bought seed compost. Avoid garden soil because it contains fungi and bugs that can harm your plants. Make sure that the compost is free of lumps as these obstruct the roots, hindering growth.

It is worth mixing some perlite or vermiculite in with the compost as this helps to retain moisture and prevents the soil from getting too wet. I typically add about 25% vermiculite and then mix it in thoroughly.

Perlite and vermiculite are not the same, but have similar properties. Perlite is a volcanic rock whereas vermiculite is mineral mined from the earth. Perlite retains less moisture than vermiculite, but does help improve drainage and aeration of the soil. If a plant prefers a drier soil, then perlite is best. Vermiculite retains more water than perlite and for longer. As well as absorbing moisture, it also absorbs nutrients that it can release over time. Plants that prefer a moist soil, should have vermiculite added to the potting mix. Either can be used with chillies, with perlite being better for hotter chillies as they prefer a drier soil.

Fill the pot with potting compost to half an inch or about 1cm from the top or fill multi-cell seed trays to very close to the top. Gently press down the compost to firm it slightly, but careful not to compact it too much. Then lightly water the compost, but do not soak it.

Put a single chilli seed in the middle of each pot or cell. Cover with a light sprinkling of compost or vermiculite and firm down again, but gently. Use a spray bottle or a watering can with a very fine rose to water the seeds in. Avoid watering too much or using a watering can without a very fine rose as this can wash the seed away or at least to the top of the compost where it then can have problems germinating.

Put labels in the pots, so you know which seedling is which variety. As the seedlings grow, they will all look the same, and you won't be able to tell the difference until the plant fruits.

A heated propagator is ideal for germinating chillies as you can keep the seeds at a constant temperature. However, remember to keep the compost moist as they can dry out quickly in the heat. This is probably the most reliable method of germinating chilli seeds and if you are serious about growing chillies, I strongly recommend you invest in a couple of these, depending on how many chillies you are planning on growing.

Alternatively, you can cover the pots or trays with plastic wrap. This creates a mini-greenhouse, helping to retain moisture and heat. Make sure you keep a close eye on the pots as the plastic wrap needs removing or at least loosening after germination to prevent mould from forming.

The seeds do not need light at this point, so you can store them in an airing cupboard until they germinate. What they do need is warmth and, in particular, bottom heat. If you are not using a heated propagator, put your seeds in your airing cupboard or somewhere that has a consistent, warm temperature. The seeds can be put on a sunny windowsill, but be careful they do not get too cold at night and are not in a draft. Chilli seedlings like a temperature of between 27-32°C/80-90°F to germinate. Remember, this is more important for the hotter varieties of chilli. Germination can still occur at temperatures as low as 21°C/70°F but will be much less reliable. As the temperature approaches 38°C/100°F, germination will be much quicker but less successful.

Keep the compost moist during germination, but not soggy. If the soil is too wet, then there is the risk of the seeds rotting.

Check the seeds every day, around the same time if you can. Watch the seeds for germination, but be patient. It can take up to a month for the hotter varieties to germinate, though most varieties will germinate in a couple of weeks. Once you see the seeds sprouting, move the pots to somewhere with bright light such as a conservatory or windowsill. Now the seedlings need plenty of light to grow, but make sure the night time temperatures are not too low. On windowsills, there is a risk of the temperature dropping low enough to harm your seedlings. Make sure that no part of the plants touches the glass as the temperature differential can be harmful to the baby plants.

Chilli seedlings emerging under grow lamps

If your seedlings do not have enough light, they will be weak and pale. The stems will become very long, the leaves small and they lean towards the light. Should your plants lean, then turn them around once or twice a day to prevent them from growing too leggy and to encourage them to grow evenly. If you are serious about your chillies, then they will benefit at this stage from grow lamps to provide consistent light levels through the day.

Should you end up with spindly chillies, you can replant them with the stem deeper when you re-pot them. Move them to a position with more constant light, and they should recover and grow into normal plants. The risk with plants that grow too leggy is that they cannot recover and grow properly.

Once your chilli seedlings have got two sets of true leaves, then they can be transplanted and put them in larger pots so they can continue to grow. This is easiest to do if your chillies are in multi-cell containers or single pots.

Transplanting Your Chilli Plants

When your seedlings have a few sets of leaves, it is time to pot them on, i.e., move them to larger pots so they can grow in comfort. If they are not transplanted, then the roots become restricted which can prevent the plant growing properly and impact the yield later in the year. When transplanting, be very careful not to damage either the roots or the leaves. This is one reason why I recommend planting chillies in multi-cell containers or single pots. When you sow a bunch of seeds together, the roots of the young plants get intertwined, and it can be difficult to untangle them without causing damage. Although the root damage is often not fatal, it can stunt the growth of the plant and potentially stop it from producing chillies. The same goes for the leaves; it is very hard to allow the plants to grow to a size where you can safely transplant them when they are all squashed together in a growing tray.

Once the plants have grown a few inches tall, they need to be moved to larger pots so that they have the room to grow and continue to develop. Failure to move them can mean the roots do not develop properly and the plant ends up being weaker and late in producing fruit. If you have started your seeds in a seed tray, then move them when they have two sets of true levels into 3"/7cm pots. If you started your seeds in this size pot, then replant them into larger pots.

Fill the pots almost to the top with fresh compost and give it a sprinkle of water to dampen the compost. Make a well in the centre of the pot that is big enough for the new seedling. If the seedling is in a pot, then make it the same size as the pot the seedling is currently in. Fit the pot into the hole to make sure that it is the right size.

Chilli seedling potted on to larger pot, under grow lamps

Carefully remove the seedling from its pot or seed tray, paying particular attention to the roots to keep disturbance to a minimum. Put the seedling into the new pot at the same depth as it was in the original pot. If your seedlings are spindly, plant them deeper so that some of the stem is underground. Peppers, like tomatoes, will grow new roots on the stems if they are buried in the soil. This helps the plant recover from being leggy and become stronger.

Firm the soil around the seedling, being careful not to damage the stem. Once it is firmly in place, give it another sprinkle or water and put the pot somewhere hot.

As your plants grow, they need replanting into bigger and bigger pots, unless you are planting them in the ground outside or a greenhouse. A typical pot size progression is 3"/7cm, 6"/15cm, and 8"/20cm. The bigger the pot, the bigger your plant will grow. Take into account the length of your growing season as if you keep repotting the plant, it will keep growing foliage and may not produce a large crop of chillies. In colder climates, growers often do not pot their chillies on into very large pots because they need them to concentrate on producing fruit rather than growing larger in size.

When the plant has flowered, feed it once or twice a week with a good general purpose liquid fertiliser such as a tomato feed. As the plants grow bigger, you can feed them more often to encourage fruit development, though be careful not to overwater the plants. Pinching out the growing tips encourages bushier growth and fruit production. Using a high nitrogen feed will encourage the plant to produce more greenery, so avoid fertilisers that are high in nitrogen and use one designed to encourage fruit production.

Planting out a chilli plant

To fruit successfully, the plants need lots of sun and warmth plus shelter from wind and extreme weather. Water and feed the plants regularly for best results. Chillies do not respond well to irregular watering as they are thirsty plants. Little and often is better than too much occasionally. If the leaves start to drop, then that is usually them telling you they are thirsty and urgently need water. Chillies need to be able to access oxygen from its roots, and overwatering prevents them from getting the oxygen they need to thrive. While stressing the chilli with a lack of water can produce hotter chillies, doing this while the plant is growing can prevent it from producing chillies at all. Chillies, like a lot of plants, drop flowers and fruit in stressful situations so that the parent plant can survive.

Caring for Your Plants

Once you have transplanted your plants, you need to take good care of them, so they not only grow to maturity, but they also produce a good crop of healthy, and perhaps hot, chillies. The hotter varieties of chillies require a lot more babying than the milder varieties and are a lot more sensitive to variations in their environment. Following these instructions ensures your plants thrive and produce a good crop.

Remember that chilli plants grown in containers are completely dependent on you for food and water, so you have to take extra care of these plants as they are less forgiving of neglect.

Light Requirements

Chilli plants thrive in full sun outdoors, so if you are planning on growing them indoors, they will need a lot of light. To get a really good crop of chillies indoors, you will need grow lights to provide the plants with enough light. However, if you have a sunny conservatory, then there may well be enough natural light for the plants.

When grown indoors, chillies require 12-16 hours of light (photoperiod) during the day and a dark (night) period of 8-12 hours. Strong light ensures strong vegetative growth and more flowers, while the amount of light (photoperiod) determines how fast your chilli plant grows.

Different types of chillies require different light levels to produce a crop. Jalapeno peppers can be grown under fluorescent grow lights and produce plenty of vegetative growth, but few fruits. Under the same conditions, a Thai chilli pepper, which needs less intense light to fruit, will produce a bountiful crop.

When using grow lights, there is a misconception that plants need constant light. Chillies, like most plants, benefit from at least some darkness every day, though the production of fruit does not depend on the length of the day. Therefore, whether the chilli plant gets 12, 18 or 24 hours of light, it will still produce flowers, though when you go over 16 hours of light there are diminishing returns, i.e. the cost of the lights do not justify the marginal increase in fruit production. Indoor growers report that a 16 hour photoperiod is the sweet spot for maximum yield from chilli peppers.

Chilli plants cannot get enough of light, remember they come from a tropical area. However, if you are moving them from indoors to outdoors, they will need some hardening off to allow them to get used to the intensity of the sunlight. When moving the plants indoors, they need a period of adjustment to get used to the heat from grow lights.

Chilli seeds, however, do not need light to germinate and will sprout in darkness. As soon as the sprouts appear, they must be moved to a light location such as a south facing window or be put under grow lights. The benefit of grow lights on seeds does not come from the light, but from the extra heat from the lights that keeps the soil warm.

For most home growers, there are two types of grow lights to consider. The established fluorescent lights and the newer, more efficient LED lights.

Fluorescent lights are often used simply because they are readily available and many people will have some in their home somewhere. These lights are cheap and quite efficient, though their light is a lower intensity than that generated by LED lights. They are good for starting seedlings and for overwintering plants.

LED lights are a newer technology and rapidly advancing. Prices have come down significantly in recent years and they are very energy efficient, making them a popular choice among growers. While LED lights can be more expensive than fluorescent lights, they last for many more years.

With the right lighting, you can grow chilli plants indoors throughout the year, easily keeping them alive through winter so they produce a good crop the following year. Chilli plants are perennials, so will live for many years when properly cared for.

Temperature Requirements

Chillies like warm temperatures, but the perfect temperature depends on the type of plant and what stage of growth it is in.

For germination to occur, chillies require a temperature of between 22-26°C/71-79°F. When the temperature drops below 20°C/68°F, germination becomes problematical.

During the growth phase, the temperature requirements vary according to the native environment for the plant. Habenero chillies grow wild in the Caribbean where daytime temperatures of 30°C/86°F are common and night time temperatures rarely drop below 19°C/66°F. The humidity level in the Caribbean is high, usually around 70%.

Capsicum pubenscens plants like a clear difference between day and night temperatures. Both *Capsicum annuum* and *Capsicum frutescens* like it warm, though plants in these families like conditions that mimic their native environment. The closer you can keep the growing environment to that of the chilli's natural habitat, the more comfortable the plants will be and the more successful your harvest will be.

When the temperature drops below 16°C/60°F, *Capsicum annuum* plants stop growing. For them, a temperature of around 26°C/79°F is perfect with a soil temperature of between 18-22°C/64-72°F is best. The plant suffers from cold damage when the temperature drops below 6°C/43°F. *Capsicum frutescens* plants have similar requirements.

Capsicum pubescens germinates well at 20°C/68°F and is the only chilli plant that tolerates a light frost, being able to survive at temperatures as low as 0°C/32°F.

Capsicum baccatum is somewhere in the middle of *C. annuum* and *C. pubescens* as this family originated in Peru where temperatures of 20-30°C/68-86°F are common. These plants don't tend to like it when the temperature falls become 15°C/59°F.

Capsicum chinense loves hot weather with daytime temperatures of 30°C/86°F in its native environment being normal. In the night, temperatures drop to around 23°C/73°F. When the temperature goes above 3°3C/91°F, pollination becomes problematical for this variety.

Temperatures below 14°C/57°F start to cause problems for pollination as when it is too cold, the female reproductive organs inside the flower cannot open properly.

In general, keeping the temperature of your growing environment at 20°C/68°F is good enough for most chilli plants. Most will tolerate some variation in this, particularly if the temperature drops a couple of degrees, but will not tolerate too great a dip in temperature.

If you are in doubt about the growing conditions of a chilli pepper, look up where it originated from and create similar growing conditions with light, heat and humidity.

Fertilising

Feeding your plants is extremely important, and there are a lot of different options for you, depending on the type of chilli you are growing, the climate and whether they are growing in pots or the ground.

You have a lot of options when it comes to how and when you fertilise (feed) your chilli peppers. As you gain experience growing chilli peppers, you will develop your own methods based on your specific climate, growing environment, soil conditions and more. Most chilli varieties have similar fertiliser requirements, though expert growers will feed super-hot chillies slightly differently.

The feeding schedule can be a bit complex, particularly when you are first starting out growing chillies. I will share a simple to follow feeding program that will ensure you have healthy chilli plants that produce a good yield.

Why Feed Your Chillies

Feeding your chillies is vital for their healthy growth, particularly as you are likely growing them in pots. The seeds have enough energy to allow the embryonic leaves, or cotyledons, to survive and appear. After this, the seeds have exhausted their energy and the plant will wither and die without more food. Your potting soil will give the plant some food, but this is usually exhausted in a few weeks, less with poor quality compost.

Once this food is gone, your plants need an external source of food and are dependent on you to provide it. When you feed your plants well, they grow healthy, green leaves (though a few varieties do have different coloured leaves) thick stems, plenty of flowers and abundant fruit.

The First Feeding

When the first set of true leaves appear, start to feed your plants. Use a fish and seaweed fertiliser or a fish emulsion. These are particularly high in micronutrients and are an excellent food source for chillies. Read the instructions on the container and dilute the fertiliser to quarter strength. At full strength, it will be too strong and potentially harmful to your seedlings.

Foliar Feeding

Once your plants have four sets of true leaves, you can begin to apply a foliar feed to your plants. This is where you use a spray bottle to spray fertiliser onto the leaves and stem.

Use Epsom salts (magnesium sulphate) as this keeps the leaves strong and prevents the deep green leaves from turning yellow, which you often see in young plants. Make sure that your Epsom salts do not have any additives in them such as bath crystals, essential oils or perfumes.

Dilute one teaspoon of Epsom salt in a gallon of water and shake well, so it mixes properly. Put this into a spray bottle, and then spray the plant until the leaves and stems are covered with the mixture.

Use the foliar feed every other week. So one week you feed your plants with a liquid fertiliser and then, on the second week, you also apply the foliar feed. This will ensure your plants grow strong and healthy.

Feeding Outdoor Peppers

If you are keeping your peppers in a container, then continue the above feeding schedule but with half strength fertiliser (salts from the fertiliser can build up in the soil and harm the plant, though this isn't as great a problem if you are also regularly using normal water). However, if you are planting your chillies outside, then continue the same feeding program, but with full strength fertiliser.

But you can also help your outdoor chillies by providing a mulch of good quality compost around each plant. This will fertilise your plants, help retain moisture and deter pests. Before you plant your chillies outside, put a good handful of compost in each hole and then place your chilli plant on top of this.

Extra Nutrient Requirements
Many growers will feed their plants with something that provides extra calcium and phosphorus, such as bonemeal. These extra nutrients help your plants become stronger, keeps them flowering and fruiting and helps to prevent blossom end rot.

If any of your plants develop bubbly or crinkly leaves, particularly the *Capsicum chinense* varieties, or if the chillies themselves develop dark, sunken lesions, then your plant is telling you it needs more calcium and phosphorous.

Follow the instructions on the label of the bonemeal to apply this to your plant. Applying this once a month is usually sufficient for chillies.

Using Compost Teas
Another good way of feeding your plants and ensuring a good yield is to use something called compost tea. This is a concentrated liquid made from good quality compost that is full of beneficial microbes that are excellent for both your plant and the soil.

Compost tea is easy to make at home. Fill a bucket about a third full with a good quality compost, either home-made or store-bought. Top up the bucket with water and stir well. Cover and leave for three or four days, stirring a few times each day. Strain the mixture through cheesecloth, burlap or any other porous material. Keep the liquid as this is the concentrating feed and dispose of the solids on your compost pile.

Dilute the liquid at a ratio of about 10:1 with normal water until it is a light brown colour, similar to a weak cup of tea. Use it straight away as it doesn't keep for more than a day or two at most as the beneficial bacteria gets killed off by the anaerobic environment.

Compost tea can be used as a foliar feed, or it can be applied directly to the soil. If you do this a couple of times each month, then it will help your plants remain strong and healthy, as well as combat diseases.

Overfeeding is Dangerous
Be careful not to feed your chillies too much. Overfeeding your plants is just as dangerous to them as underfeeding them and can kill them. Always follow the instructions on the fertiliser label for the quantity and strength to use, particularly with liquid fertilisers. If the mixture is too strong, it can burn the leaves of the plant. If you notice the edges of the leaves starting to turn brown, then this is most likely an indication of fertiliser burn. Stop feeding the plants and reduce the amount you are feeding them.

If your plants are in the soil or containers outside, then you can flush the excess fertiliser out of the soil by running water through the soil. Afterward, leave the plants plenty of time to dry out thoroughly before watering again.

Watering

Watering chilli plants is just as important as feeding them, particularly when growing in containers. It is hard to determine a precise schedule as it depends on a wide variety of factors ranging from the environment, the soil, the size of the plant, the weather and more.

As a general rule of thumb, watering little and often is best for chilli plants. The top of the soil can often look dry, but an inch or two under the surface, the soil is much damper. If you only check the top of the soil, you can end up overwatering your plants as you think they are dry. This is just as bad as not watering them at all.

As many chillies originate in an area that is hot and dry, water is not always available so the plants can survive quite well without water. Often they will look withered and unwell after a day of heat and no water, yet after a good drink, they very quickly perk back up again. Most varieties are relatively drought tolerant, though it is best to keep water levels even when the plant is flowering to avoid flower drop.

Top or Bottom Watering
Because of the environment these plants originated in, they do not get a large amount of rain, so they do not respond as well to being watered from above. Chillies are best watered from below, which more closely simulates their natural environment. Therefore, if you are growing in pots, have saucers underneath them that you can add water to and let the plants suck the water up. However, do not leave the plants to sit in water for long periods of time

as that isn't good for them either.

If you are growing in the ground outdoors, water at the base of the plant at night and avoid getting water on the leaves. This lets the water and nutrients from any fertiliser soak into the soil down to the roots where the plant can draw them up in the morning.

In hot areas, if you water in the morning, much of the water can evaporate before it gets down to the roots of your chilli plants. If you are fertilising your plants at the same time, then the water can evaporate, leaving a salty nutrient layer in the top of the soil which is also bad for your plants. In hotter climates, water in the evenings, direct to the base of the plant, or push a tube into the soil at the base of each plant to pour water down to avoid surface evaporation.

Fungus Gnats
These can be a problem when you are growing in containers as you often have little choice but to feed and water the plant from the top. This, unfortunately, creates a perfect breeding ground for a wide variety of insects, including the annoying fungus gnat. These are found on dead plant matter and near water and leave their eggs near the roots of the plants, which their young then feed on.

These gnats breed like crazy and, in large quantities, can cause some damage to the plant from their activity at the roots.

Should you end up with an infestation, remove the plant from the pot, run water over the roots to wash away the soil and gnat eggs. Then shake gently to remove any soil that is left and then repot into fresh compost and start feeding/watering from the bottom.

When you grow in the ground, these insects are not so much of a problem because there are natural predators that keep their numbers down.

Using Municipal Tap Water
The water that comes out of your kitchen taps contains the chemical chlorine, which is added to kill disease-causing bacteria, making it safe to drink. While the levels of chlorine have minimal effect on you and me, plants cannot process it. When feeding your chilli plants with tap water, you may find salty deposits left behind in the plant's veins, which will turn the leaves yellow. Ideally, use rain water as it does not have chlorine in, but it may not always be possible to do this.

This yellowing of the leaves then affects the efficiency of the photosynthesis process, which, in turn, affects the growth of the plant and ultimately, the yield.

Fill a bucket with water and leave it overnight for the chlorine to evaporate away. This prevents the yellow effect you get on the leaves, and you end up with nice, green leaves on the plants. Unfortunately, once a leaf has turned yellow, it is very unlikely to recover as the plant cannot remove the chlorine from itself.

The Dangers of Overwatering

Overwatering a plant is just as bad for it as underwatering it. When you give a plant too much water, you end up removing the air from the soil, which reduces or removes the amount of oxygen available to the roots.

Plants need oxygen as much as we do and use it to transport nutrients around its system, including the vital sugar that is created during photosynthesis. A lack of oxygen means that the plant cannot transport essential nutrients around itself and so its growth is stunted and the harvest diminished.

When there is not enough oxygen, nutrients build up in the soil as the plant does not have the energy to use the nutrients effectively.

The pH Value of Water

Your municipal tap water is usually slightly alkaline, with a pH in the region of 7.0 to 8.0. However, plants prefer a more acidic pH level, similar to what would occur in rainfall, somewhere from pH 5.0 through to 6.0.

Unless you are growing to compete in competitions or to break the world record for the hottest chilli, rainwater or tap water will be okay for your plants.

However, if you are really serious about your chillies, then test the pH level of any water you are using. Adjust the pH level to between 5.0 and 6.0 by dripping in a little acid. This will give your plants the best possible growing conditions.

Seriously Hot Chillies

To get very hot chilli plants, you need to give them a little bit of abuse! Chillies that grow in a comfortable environment with plenty of water tend not to be as hot as they could be. It seems that limiting the availability of water to your plants helps to make the chillies even hotter!

Be careful not to give your plants so little water that they struggle to produce fruit. But give them less water than you would otherwise and they will concentrate on making the chilli fruits even hotter.

Pruning

Chilli plants do not need to be pruned if you are growing them as annuals. If you are overwintering them and keeping them for more than a year, then pruning is a good idea to keep the plant healthy and growing well.

When pruning your chilli plants, do not remove the growing tip as this is not good for the plant. Take out side shoots and branches that are rubbing, opening up the plant to allow the air to circulate. This helps reduce the chances of disease and ensures that the plant can continue to grow healthily. If you are growing outside, pruning helps the plants survive high winds and produce strong stems that can support larger yields of chillies.

Pruning creates bushier plants that branch out and create more flowers, which results in a greater yield. When you prune at the beginning of the season, i.e., at the start of summer, the quality of the peppers on the plant improve. Pruning later in the season helps ripen any chillies left on the plant before the frosts arrive. Chillies grown in containers benefit from a good pruning later in the season, which allows you overwinter the plant and give it a head start on the following year.

Early Season Pruning

The process for early season pruning is relatively easy and is as follows:

1. Chilli plants tend to grow in a 'Y' shape with a bottom stem and then two main branches.
2. Follow one of the main branches up from its base to the first small branch that comes of the side of it. Clip this branch off using sharp scissors.
3. Continue up the branch, count three more side shoots and cut off the third shoot. Cut off every third side branch on the main branch. Alternate between the inner and outer branches.
4. Repeat this process on the other main branch which will balance out the plant. You are making sure that the branches do not cross or touch as you improve air circulation.

Late Season Pruning

The process for late season pruning is:

1. Start at the bottom of one of the main branches. Find the first side shoot that has no peppers or flowers on. Clip this branch off using sharp scissors.
2. Continue up the main branch, removing any side shoots that are not productive. Allow at least half of the branches to remain on the plant which will let it continue to grow.
3. Repeat the process on the other main branch, allowing the plant to focus its energy on ripening the rest of the peppers.

How To Make Chillies Hotter

It is possible to make chilli plants produce fruit that are slightly hotter than normal. Using these steps, you can ensure any chilli you grow is on the hotter end of the spectrum.

The first step is to choose a variety of chilli that produces hot peppers. Carolina reaper is the obvious choice, but there are many other varieties on the market that are very hot. Get the seeds from a reputable supplier so that you know you are getting the right seeds.

Water Slightly Less

If your plants get slightly less water than normal, then this will cause the fruits to be hotter than normal. This won't turn a jalapeno into a Carolina reaper, but it will make sure the fruits are on the hotter end of the scale for that pepper. Be careful not to underwater the plants to a degree where they drop fruit and flowers. Wait until the plant has started to set fruit and then when the leaves start to look a little droopy, give it some water. This stress helps the plant produce hotter peppers.

Lower Nitrogen Levels

If chillies get too much nitrogen, it will concentrate on producing leaves rather than fruit, so to get more fruit that is hotter, feed using a fertiliser lower in nitrogen and higher in potassium and phosphorus. A fertiliser such as well-rotted compost or manure is ideal as it does not contain too much nitrogen. When the blossoms first appear, side dress the plant with well-rotted compost or manure, then repeat three weeks later to give the plant a boost. Spraying the leaves with a dilute solution of Epsom salts (one teaspoon of Epsom salt to one litre/one quart water) will also help to promote fruiting. Keen growers recommend using a liquid seaweed feed three or four times on chilli plants over the course of the growing season.

Add Sulphur

Adding sulphur to the soil of chilli plants benefits the plant as well as helps to produce hotter peppers. While you can buy bags of sulphur, some gardeners will put unlit matches in the soil before planting as the match heads contain sulphur. It is a much cheaper alternative than buying sulphur itself. Sulphur can be applied as a top dressing or mixed into the soil.

Epsom salt is very good for chilli plants because it is hydrated magnesium sulphate. It is around 10% magnesium and 13% sulphur. Magnesium benefits your plants as it helps the absorb nutrients better and create chlorophyll. Sulphur assists in photosynthesis, helps the plant grow and improves disease resistance. Epsom salts can be bought from most chemists or online.

Apply Epsom salts as a foliar spray by diluting two tablespoons of Epsom salt in a gallon/4.5 litre water and shake well. Fill a spray bottle with this mixture, then mist the leaves of your plants until they are dripping wet. Do this once a month instead of watering your chilli plants.

Alternatively, Epson salts can be applied by watering where a tablespoon of Epsom salt is dissolved in 1 gallon/4.5 litre of water and then the plant is watered well. Repeat every 3-4 weeks.

Apply as a side dressing at a ratio of one tablespoon of Epsom salt per 12"/30cm of plant height. Sprinkle this around the base of each plant every 4 or 5 weeks. Start side dressing your plants when the first true leaves start to appear.

When transplanting chilli plants, add one or two tablespoons of Epsom salts to each hole, then cover the salt with soil so that roots do not come into direct contact with the salt. Adding Epsom salt to your potting compost helps to improve germination rates and ensure health seedlings.

Cross Pollination

Chilli plants can cross pollinate with each other and even with sweet, bell peppers. This makes the seeds of the next generation of chillies much milder than expected. Therefore, different varieties of peppers should be grown a good distance from each other or grown in such a way that cross pollination is not possible. In this case, hand pollinate your plants to ensure you maintain the heat in the chillies.

Allow Peppers To Age On The Plant

As chillies age on the plant, so they will become hotter as the capsaicin levels increase over time. Therefore, if you can wait until green peppers turn red, you end up with much hotter peppers. However, this needs to be balanced with your need to harvest the peppers. As you know, harvesting the peppers encourages the plant to produce more.

Stress Your Peppers
Interestingly, stressing chilli plants (without harming them too much) increases the capsaicin levels in the fruit. This is surprisingly simple to do and can be done by snapping off a few stems, fruits or leaves. This imitates harm caused by animals or insects in the wild, which encourages the plant to make the fruits hotter to protect them and make them less attractive as food.

Growing Chillies In A Greenhouse

In temperate zones, chillies are best grown in a greenhouse as the weather outside is generally not warm enough for them to thrive and produce a healthy crop. If you do not have a full sized greenhouse, then a smaller, plastic greenhouse will be suitable. Just remember to space the plants properly and to fix the greenhouse down well as these are light and easily damaged in high winds.

In a greenhouse, chillies are sown from January through to March and harvested from August through to as late as November, depending on your local climate and the chilli cultivar.

Most chilli plants are sown from February through to late March or early April. Hotter varieties generally require a longer growing season, so benefit from being sown earlier in the year. However, this is dependent on whether or not you have the equipment or environment for them to thrive during these colder months.

The seeds are started as described in the previous section. They do benefit from being started in plastic propagators for extra protection from the elements and to provide a little bit more heat. If you have a heated greenhouse, then it is much easier to start chilli seeds off early, but if not, then it can be better to leave them until March when the temperatures are higher and germination a little easier.

Around late April to early May, the chilli seedlings will be ready to be planted into 20-25cm/8-10" pots in their final position. You can put the plants into the ground in a greenhouse if you prefer. Chilli plants benefit from being tied into a bamboo cane to provide some support. Put the cane in the pot as early as possible to avoid damage to the root structure. When the plants reach 20-25cm/8-10" tall, pinch out the growing tip to encourage side shoots and bushier growth.

Keep the plants well watered, particularly during hot weather as they will dry out very quickly in containers. At the height of summer, you may need to water the plants a couple of times a day. Make sure the windows and vents of your greenhouse are open to allow for the air to circulate too. It is worth spraying the chilli plant leaves with water as this helps deter pests such as red spider mites.

The one problem you can have in a greenhouse is pollination as insects may not find their way to your plants. Having pots of flowers in your greenhouse and leaving the door open will help, but even so, pollination can be unreliable. The best approach is to use a small, soft paintbrush and hand pollinating your plants, taking care not to cross pollinate different varieties.

Over the summer as they ripen, the fruit will turn from green to red, in most cases. Generally, the longer you leave them, the hotter the chillies become. However, regular harvesting of the chillies encourages more fruits to form.

Growing in a greenhouse is best in temperate climates purely because the growing season isn't long enough outside and the weather not reliable enough, for chilli plants to mature fully outdoors.

.

HARVESTING CHILLIES

With most chilli plants, you can harvest the fruit at almost any time. A lot of varieties can be harvested before they are fully ripe, when they are green and at any time until they are completely ripe and have turned red. Of course, it depends on the variety as to what colour the ripe fruit is.

Harvesting some of the fruit before it is ripe is a good idea because it encourages the plant to produce more fruit. When the chillies are ripe, remove them from the plant straight away rather than leaving them on it. This also encourages the plant to continue producing fruit for longer. Remember that depending on the climate where you live, the chillies may not ripen all the way to red, so you may have to harvest them before they are fully ripe.

Chillies in various stages of maturity

Should you get to the end of the growing season and still have unripe chillies, they can be ripened off the plant similarly to how tomatoes are ripened. Put the chillies in a paper bag with a ripe banana, and this encourages the fruit to ripen. Ripe bananas give off ethylene which ripens other fruits or vegetables placed near them. You can also fleece your chilli plants towards the end of the season which helps retain heat and encourage the fruit to continue to ripen.

Once harvested, store in your refrigerator or use in one of the many recipes found later in this book. Chilli jam and sauce are popular ways to store a lot of chillies, or you can dry them for use later in the year or to create your very own chilli powder blend.

Saving Your Chilli Seeds

When you grow a variety of chilli that you particularly like, or if you find some in the store that you'd like to grow, you can save the seeds and grow plants from them the following year.

Be aware though, that capsaicin oil, which is the burning hot component of a chilli, is highly concentrated in the placenta (white ribs) that holds the seeds. This is hard to remove from your skin and will burn your eyes, nose, mouth and many other parts of your body where burning would not be pleasant. If you are dealing with anything hotter than a bell pepper, I'd strongly recommend wearing thin plastic gloves to prevent the possibility of getting capsaicin oil on your body. Trust me, it burns bad with the hotter chillies, and it is a mistake you are only ever going to make once, you learn very quickly!

For chillies that are extremely hot, I recommend wearing plastic safety goggles as well. I am serious, when you cut into a chilli, oil can squirt up into your eyes, or you can unconsciously rub your eyes, even with plastic gloves on and that could end up with a trip to the emergency room.

Should an accident happen, and you get chilli oil anywhere, do not rub the affected area but keep it cool with cold compresses. Applying yogurt or milk can help counteract the effect of the capsaicin oil, though it takes a little time to work. Capsaicin oil in your eyes or nose is very painful but fortunately will wear off over time.

Selecting the Best Pods for Viable Seeds
You will have more chance of your seeds germinating if you choose the best possible seeds from your plants. Look for pods that are completely ripe,

remembering that it will take a few months for the pods to completely mature. Do not choose any pods that are diseased or infected by pests. If your plant has a disease, then you should think twice about saving the seeds from it just in case they are carrying the disease.

The pod is fully mature when it has reached its final colour. Which colour this is depends on the variety of chilli you are growing, which is usually detailed on the packet, can be found online or in the section on chilli varieties earlier in this book. Usually, it is red, but some cultivars mature to different colours. Immature pods are very unlikely to provide seeds that will germinate successfully.

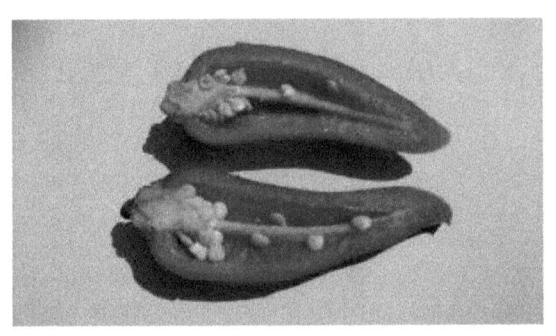

If your chilli pods are funny shapes, don't worry, you can still use the seeds. The genetics of the plant should still be fine, and the seeds will produce healthy plants. Just avoid saving seeds from any pods that are rotten, mouldy or diseased. Some diseases and viruses can be passed on to future generations of the plant, so these are best avoided to ensure healthy plants.

Removing and Drying Seeds
Before storing the seeds, you have to ensure they are fully dry. If they retain moisture, then the seeds may sprout prematurely, or they become mouldy in storage and are no longer be viable or damage all of your saved seeds.

Generally, the moisture content must be below 8%. You may find this a little hard to measure, but the general rule of thumb is that the seeds need to be brittle. If they are not and bend when you press them, then they need to be dried further until they are solid.

Dry seeds in a dehydrator, by leaving them on a piece of kitchen towel or a paper plate until they are thoroughly dried out.

Firstly, remove the seeds carefully from the pod, cutting out the membrane using a sharp knife. Then pick the seeds off by hand, leaving none of the placentae on the seed. Any seeds that are damaged or discoloured are discarded.

Dry the seeds somewhere warm, but not in direct sunlight. An airing cupboard, if you have one, is ideal. Lay the seeds out in a single layer so they are not touching on a paper tray or plate. Every few days, turn the seeds to make sure they dry fully. Wherever you are drying your seeds, ensure there is good airflow, which helps the seeds dry evenly.

After about seven to ten days, the seeds should be dry. Try to bend one of the seeds. If it does bend, then it is not dry enough and needs to be left longer. Seeds that are fully dry are brittle and if you try to bite them, will not dent.

Storing Seeds
Only store the seeds when they are fully dry. The seeds will store for a year and often much longer when they are completely dry, providing they are stored somewhere with a constant temperature and that is dry. Over time, the germination rate will fall, so it is best to use your dried seeds within a couple of years or to store them to ensure their viability.

When you store your seeds, make sure you label them with the name of the variety as well as the date you stored them. I'd also recommend recording useful information such as where you got the original seeds from and the germination rate of the original batch of seeds. These will help you keep track of your seeds and know where they have come from.

Store seeds in a cool, dark place that is dry. The ideal temperature is between 1-10°C/35-50°F. I wrap my seeds in paper towels, then put them in plastic ziplock bags in a plastic container in the bottom of my fridge. This simulates the cold, dark conditions of winter and slows the metabolism of the seeds so that when you remove them to plant them, they burst into life as they think they have slept through winter.

Correctly storing your seeds is very important as if you do not ensure they are thoroughly dry and stored properly, they can rot or fail to germinate. Remember to label the seeds so that you know which seeds are which, as it's impossible to tell the variety by looking at the seeds. The seeds should be viable for several years if stored correctly, though, over time, the germination rate will drop which is natural and to be expected.

You can dry seeds from the chilli plants you grow or from chilli pods that you buy in stores. Seeds cannot be saved from pods that have been dried, cooked, pickled or otherwise processed. This is a great way to grow a variety that you enjoyed again without having to buy more seeds. When you buy the more expensive varieties such as Carolina Reaper or other rare cultivars, this is a significant money saving exercise.

Overwintering Chilli Plants

Chilli plants will produce a good crop in their first year, though they produce larger harvests in the second and even third year. Overwintering is where you shelter a tender plant from cold weather and low light levels so it can survive through to the following year. Due to the poor growing conditions in most temperate climates, chilli plants barely grow between October and January/February time.

The other big advantage of overwintering a chilli plant is that it has a head start when the light levels increase in the spring. The result is a larger crop, often maturing earlier than it did in the first year as it effectively has a longer growing season.

As a general rule of thumb, *Capsicum pubescens* varieties overwinter much better than varieties in the *Capsicum annum* family.

Only overwinter your strongest plants that are pest and disease free. The weaker plants are much less likely to survive the winter or succumb to the cooler conditions.

Pick all the fruit from the plant, including immature ones. If there are still unripe fruits, then you can either use them in that condition or ripen them off the plant.

Next, prune the plant. This is going to require you to be very brave as you are removing all the side shoots, leaving the main stem and two or three inches of each of the main 'Y' stems. All the other shoots are cut off, leaving behind a stick. Yes, it sounds very harsh, but it helps to make sure your plant survives the winter as it goes into an almost dormant state.

Chilli plants that have been grown outside in the ground can also be overwintered in cooler areas. Simply dig them up, put them in a container and move them inside where they are out of the weather and protected from frost. Be very careful when you dig it up not to cause too much root damage. Shake off excess soil and put it in a good sized pot with fresh compost.

Your chilli plants need to be stored somewhere that is frost free, with a temperature of between 5-12°C/41-54°F. This can be a heated greenhouse, a heated propagator or on a sunny windowsill, though make sure they do not touch a window though as the temperature differential will damage the plant. Ensure there is room between the plants for the air to circulate as this prevents diseases from taking hold.

During the winter, because it is cooler and the plant does not grow very much, it require a lot less water. Check every week to see how dry the compost is and only water when it is dry. You could be watering them as little as once every three or even four weeks. Watering too much in winter creates a damp compost in which mould will breed. It can also cause the roots to rot, which will kill your plant.

When spring comes, typically late February to early March, the weather warms up, and your plants start to grow. This is when you would turn the heat up on a heated propagator and start being a little bit more vigilant in their care.

Start hardening off your plants from around the middle of April to the start of May, depending on when your last frost date is. A couple of weeks after the last frost date they will be ready to plant out and be cared for as normal. Even once the last frost date has passed, keep a close eye on the weather reports and if there is a risk of frost, cover your chilli plants to protect them as a late frost can devastate your plants.

Overwintering is a great way to preserve your best chilli plants and give them a head start the following year. It is very important that they are kept in a frost free environment as they has no frost tolerance at all. They will go dormant in cool temperatures, which is what you want, and then come back to life the following year when the temperatures warm up again. The temptation will be to think your dormant plants are dead, but they are not, and in the spring you will see new buds and leaves forming as the plant comes back to life again.

Growing Chillies in Containers

Outside of the zones where chillies grow naturally, most people grow in containers. When growing in the ground, you are limited by the growing season, meaning that you only have the time between the first and last frost for your chillies to mature and fruit.

Due to the long growing season required for chillies to mature, most people outside of the tropical and subtropical zones (USDA zones 9 to 11) grow chillies indoors or under glass in containers.

Chillies grow perfectly well in containers and can, when protected from the cold, live for a couple of years or sometimes longer. The plants need sufficient room in their containers to grow and regular feeding and watering but will thrive and produce a good crop for you.

Initially, chillies are started off in smaller pots, then moved to larger pots to grow a bit more and moved to their final container. For most varieties, a five-gallon container (around 30cm/12" wide and deep) is ideal for the final pot. Smaller varieties will be happy in three-gallon containers, and some of the larger cultivars need pots as big as ten gallons. In warmer climates where chillies thrive, they benefit from larger containers as they grow better and need more room.

In tropical or sub-tropical areas, chillies can be planted any time of the year, except during the hottest months. Everywhere else, seeds are usually sown indoors six to ten weeks before the last frost date or when the night temperatures remains above 12°C/55°F. Germination can take up to three or four weeks, and the hotter varieties require warmer, more consistent temperatures to germinate.

Once your plants have germinated and are growing, they need to be placed somewhere that gets full sun. They love heat and need to get as much sun as possible. However, you also need good air circulation so that you avoid diseases. In hotter climates, the plants benefit from shade in the afternoon to prevent damage to the pods or leaves.

When growing in containers, the soil is vital as it will keep your plants healthy and productive. Use a good quality potting mix that is loose and well drained. Cheap potting mixes tend to be full of lumps and doesn't drain very well, which will not do your chillies any good. Mix in some vermiculite or perlite which will help the soil to retain moisture and not dry out too quickly. I recommend mixing up the soil in a bucket and then filling the container to reduce the amount of spillage and mess.

The soil needs to be both free draining and water retaining. Chillies don't like the soil to get too dry, though some growers allow this to happen to stress the chillies into producing hotter pods. Check your plants daily. If you see the leaves drooping, then the plant is in need of water.

When flowers start to appear, water slightly less, but do not let the soil dry out completely. If the soil gets too dry, then the flowers will drop, resulting in no chillies. Water at the bottom of the container, i.e., into a saucer the pot stands in, or water directly to the soil. Avoid getting water onto the leaves as this can cause fungal infections.

As you are growing chillies in containers, they are completely dependent on you for food, which means regular fertilising. Most potting composts will contain enough nutrients for your chillies for anything up to several weeks. However, chillies are greedy plants and need lots of food. The best fertiliser to use is a tomato food, which chillies do very well on. Follow the instructions on the fertiliser bottle and apply at the specified intervals. Be careful of applying too much, too often as it can harm the plant and cause a build-up of salts in the soil.

When growing in containers, it is usually best not to let the chilli plant grow to its full height. Most growers pinch the growing tip out when the plant is anything from 15-30cm/6-12 inches tall to encourage the plant to grow into a bushier shape, rather than growing tall and leggy.

One thing to remember when growing in containers is that the plants still need to be supported. If they are outside, then the wind can damage the plants and sometimes the weight of fruit can tip the plant. Put a bamboo cane in the soil next to the main stem and tie the chilli to it. Depending on the height of the chilli, you may need to tie it in a several places and even support some of the branches.

Pollination occurs in the same way as normal for chillies that are grown in containers. However, be aware that if you are growing indoors or undercover, then you may need to hand pollinate your plants as insects may not be able to get to the flowers to do the job for you.

Chillies will grow to maturity in a container and are harvested as normal. Remember that if you keep harvesting the pods, the plant will continue to produce more flowers and more fruit for you. Container grown plants require more regular care than those grown in the ground because the plants are dependent on outside input to survive, i.e., you. Most people outside of the tropical and sub-tropical growing zones will grow their chillies in containers because they are growing indoors. You can get a great crop from container grown chillies and can even move the plants indoors so they can grow again next year.

Growing Chillies in a Hydroponic Environment

Another way to grow chillies, which is popular outside of their normal growing areas, is to grow them hydroponically. This is soil-free gardening where the plants are rooted in a growing medium and water. Hydroponics allows the plants to very easily access nutrients and water, meaning they grow faster and usually produce better quality crops.

Although this may sound like a panacea, it still needs work and attention from you to ensure the nutrient levels are correct. It does involve spending some money when you start out to buy all the equipment too. Hydroponics is a great way to grow chilli plants, but it is more commonly used by very dedicated growers due to the expense. New growers are better off using containers unless they are in the far north, in which case hydroponics can provide a good way to grow plants to maturity if you are willing to spend the money and have the space for the hydroponic kit.

Hydroponics has several benefits when compared to the traditional, soil-based growing methods. You do not have an issue with soil borne diseases, it is great for locations with poor quality soil or a poor growing environment, allows you to plant more densely and produces higher yields. This is a very nutrient and water efficient method of growing that is gaining popularity across the world as the cost of hydroponic systems continues to come down.

In hydroponics, a neutral substrate is used rather than soil. This is where the plant puts down its roots and allows it very efficient access to the required nutrients. The plant spends less energy on building a root system because it does not need to push through the dense soil, meaning it has more energy to focus on growth and producing fruit. As well as this, the plants need light.

This can be provided with specialist grow lamps or can be natural sunlight from a windowsill or greenhouse. Artificial light is more commonly used because it is more consistent and under your control, so the plants can have precisely the right growing environment.

A hydroponic system is made up of a container which holds the nutrient solution, a method of delivering this nutrient solution to the roots of the plant and a pump to circulate and oxygenate the nutrient solution. The exact setup depends on the type of hydroponic system you are using. Some, such as the ebb and flow system, use a growing medium, whereas others, such as the nutrient film technology (NFT) method, do not use any growing medium at all.

Hydroponic Growing Methods

There are four main systems of growing hydroponically:

1. Ebb and Flow – also known as flood and drain or intermittent flow. This is a simple solution that is a common starter set-up as it is relatively cheap to buy. The plants grow in pots with a fast draining growing medium. The roots are regularly flooded with nutrient solution and then drained, leaving air and nutrients in the roots. This system is very good for growing chillies.

EBB AND FLOW

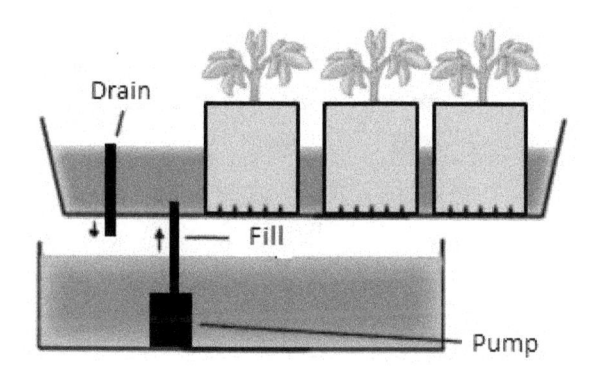

2. Continuous Flow – in these systems, the nutrient solution is delivered constantly to the roots. Drip irrigation and nutrient film technique systems fall into this category.

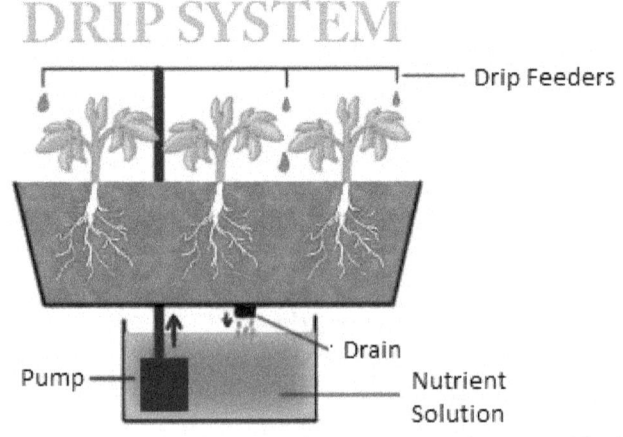

DRIP SYSTEM

3. Aquaculture – rafts float on the nutrient solution, with the roots always immersed in the water. An aerator runs to make sure the nutrient solution does not stagnate. This type of system is not particularly good for chillies, being better suited for faster-growing crops such as lettuces.

WATER CULTURE

4. Aeroponics – in this method, the plants are in net pots that hang above a container. The roots grow into the air and are regularly, or sometimes continuously, misted with the nutrient solution. This method provides a lot of oxygen to the roots which mean the plant grows very quickly. Aeroponics is another good way of growing chillies, though may be better suited to people with more experience with hydroponic systems.

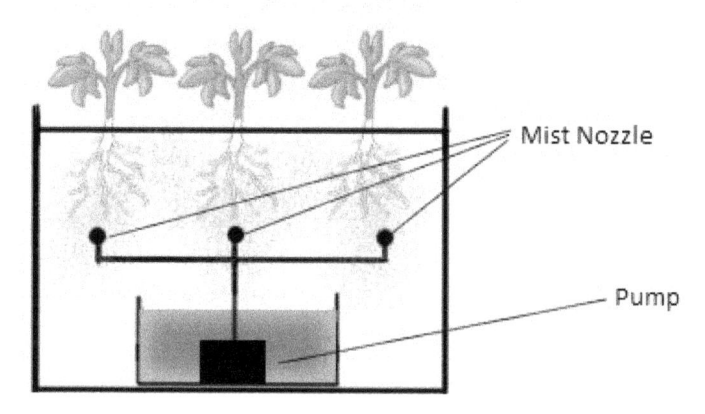

There are many different types of growing medium that you can use. This substrate is organically neutral, and its only purpose is to support the roots and hold small amounts of the nutrient solution. Some of the popular growing mediums include:

- Rockwool – made up of fibers spun from molten rock, formed into cubes or slabs. Retains moisture very well and is great for potting on. Can be used for two or three growing seasons.

- Expanded Clay Pellets – made from heat treated clay with a honeycomb structure that retains both air and moisture. Provides excellent support for your plants and can be reused many times.

- Coco Fibre – this is completely organic, being made from refined coconut husks. It has a very open texture and allows good, airy rooting. This growing medium is commonly used with pot based hydroponic systems.
- Vermiculite – a mica type material that has been heated and expanded. It retains moisture very well and is good for propagation. It is best to mix this with another growing medium to prevent possible waterlogging.
- Perlite – a lightweight, volcanic material that has been heat treated. It is often mixed with other growing mediums such as vermiculite and is used at any time in the plant's life cycle. It is good in drip irrigation and continuous flow hydroponic systems.

Nutrient Solutions

Your plants need both macro and micronutrients to grow into healthy, mature plants. You are, undoubtedly, familiar with the macronutrients which are nitrogen, phosphorus, and potassium, usually displayed on fertiliser packaging as the N-P-K ratio. As well as this, plants need micronutrients in lesser quantities to ensure healthy plant growth.

Most plants require magnesium, silicon, sulphur, and calcium as well as other minerals including manganese, iron, copper, zinc, boron and selenium, amongst others.

As your plants grow and develop, their nutrient requirements change. When starting out and growing foliage, chillies need high levels of nitrogen to encourage foliage growth. When the plant starts to flower, reduce the nitrogen levels and use more potassium and phosphorus to encourage flowering and fruit growth. Although this may sound complex, there is no more chemistry involved other than reading some packaging. Start your plants off by buying a high nitrogen nutrient solution and then, when they start to flower, replace that with a nutrient solution that has less nitrogen and more of the other two elements. Any hydroponic shop owner will be able to advise you on the best nutrients for each stage of chilli plant development.

It is possible to use one nutrient solution throughout the life cycle of your plant. Although this will work and your plant will grow, you get a better crop and a higher yield by adjusting the nutrient solution depending on what stage of growth your plants are at.

Nutrient solutions are often available as either premixed or unmixed concentrates. Unmixed means you make it up yourself following the manufacturer's instructions to ensure you get the right N-P-K ratio. Alternatively, you can buy premixed solutions with specific N-P-K ratios, though these can be a little bit more expensive.

To keep your plants healthy, you need to monitor the nutrient solution, checking for dissolved salts, temperature, and even the pH level. Again, a degree in chemistry is not required as these can all be measured using relatively cheap gadgets.

Checking Dissolved Salt Levels

It is important to regularly check the dissolved salt levels in your nutrient solution to reduce the risk of your plant's yellowing or their growth stunting due to a mineral deficiency. It is very easy to do and is calculated based on electrical conductivity.

A cF meter is used to measure the levels of dissolved salts. Put the meter in the nutrient solution and it tells you the conductivity factor (cF), usually in parts per million (PPM), though some will also measure in millisiemens per square centimetre (mS/cm2). These figures are checked against the manufacturer's instructions and the nutrient solution adjusted if required.

Every system is different, but when growing chillies, a range of 15-25cF (1.5-2.5 mS/cm2) is generally okay.

It is recommended that even when regularly checking nutrient solution levels, the system is flushed with clean water every two to three weeks to prevent a build-up of excess nutrients and to rebalance any mineral deficiencies.

Measuring the pH Level

The pH level of the nutrient solution is an indication of how acidic or alkaline it is, which affects the plant's ability to absorb nutrients from the solution. Chillies need a pH level of between 5.8 and 6.8 for optimum growth. Although they will grow outside of this pH level, they struggle if the pH strays too far from the optimum.

The pH levels are measured with litmus paper or, more commonly these days, with electronic testers, which are far easier to use. If the pH level strays from the ideal, then adjust it, but ensure that you do so gradually, as a big change in the pH level can shock your plants.

Measuring the Temperature

The temperature of the nutrient solution is kept at a constant temperature. In most cases, you don't need any heating as the plants won't mind some small temperature changes. Use a thermometer for this. If necessary, use a heater in the nutrient solution to warm it up or insulate your nutrient tank to reduce heat loss.

The nutrient solution is best kept at a temperature of between 19-21°C/66-70°F.

Lighting Requirements

As you are well aware, plants need light to grow. In a hydroponic system, the light can be provided naturally or artificially with grow lamps. The best results usually come from artificial light as most people set up their hydroponic system indoors. Mine is on top of my refrigerator, and I use artificial lights as there is not enough natural light in that area for the plants to grow properly.

Typically, the more powerful the lamp, the more energy it gives the plant. However, you need to be aware that if your plant grows too close to the lights, then they can get burned if you aren't using LED lights. Usually, the lights are raised up as the plants grow to avoid damage to the foliage from the heat.

You can use a single set of grow lamps throughout the life cycle of your chillies and the plants will grow fine. However, better results are obtained by using different types of bulbs with different spectrums and light colours for the various stages of their life cycle. Only the most serious of growers will invest in the different bulbs, with most home gardeners choosing a broad spectrum light that can be used throughout the growing season.

The plants must have a night and day cycle to their artificial lights. Use a timed switch to give the plants 12 to 16 hours of 'day' and the rest as night. Depending on the type of lights you are using, ventilation or fans may be required to circulate air and remove excess heat from the plants.

There are four main types of lighting systems:

1. LED – the cheapest of the lighting solutions, this is a relatively new technology that is advancing rapidly. LEDs are low energy and low heat, but still take care that your plants do not touch the lights as can burn or dry out the leaves. One set of LEDs will usually do for the entire plant life cycle, though you can buy light sets of different spectrums for the vegetative growth and flowering stages.

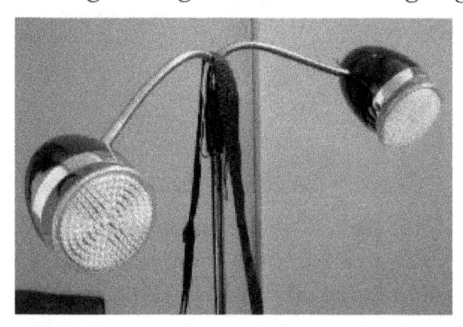

2. High-Pressure Sodium (HPS) – these produce a lot of heat, so need some form of heat removal system in place. They are also the most expensive of the light systems. You can buy general purpose bulbs that are good for any stage of growth, or you can change the bulbs during the flowering and vegetative growth stage. HPS bulbs do not have a long life and need changing every year or two.
3. Metal Halide – this type of light is great for encouraging foliage growth because it produces light that is at the blue end of the spectrum. It isn't so good for other stage of growth, being less popular these days due to the rise in LED lighting.
4. Compact Fluorescent (CFL) – these are energy efficient lights compared to the previous two types. They aren't as bright, but they are much cheaper to run and produce less heat than both sodium and metal halide. The light produced by these bulbs is more towards the blue spectrum, so better for vegetative growth.

Growing the Plants

Chilli seeds can be started out traditionally, in the soil, but the soil needs to be washed off completely before transplanting to the hydroponic environment. Alternatively, you can start chillies off in Rockwool cubes hydroponically, which works well too. You can buy small, hydroponic starter systems which are ideal for germinating seeds. Once they have germinated and are a couple of inches high, usually after about a month, move them to a full-size hydroponic system to grow to maturity.

If you have started your chillies off hydroponically, then it is very easy to transplant them. You take the small Rockwool cube and put it in a larger one.

Follow the instructions for the hydroponic system to ensure you have the right nutrient strengths. Monitor them regularly and adjust the nutrient strength as required based on how big they are. Once they start to flower, change the nutrient solution from a 'grow' nutrient to a 'bloom' nutrient with a slightly different mix of nutrients to encourage good fruit production. Makes sure to read and follow the manufacturer's instructions.

As you are most likely to be growing chillies hydroponically indoors, you will encounter fewer pests and problems. However, you will be regularly checking your plants, so if there is a problem you are going to spot it much earlier on.

Hydroponics is a very involved subject which you can find out more in my book on the subject, A Beginners Guide to Hydroponics, available online and in all good bookshops. It may sound complex, but once you get used to it, it is easy to follow and produces a good crop of chillies. The big advantage of this method of growing is that you are not tied to the growing season, making it ideal for northerly climates. The fruit is harvested as normal, and many people feel hydroponically grown chillies are tastier than soil grown ones. It is harder to stress hydroponic chillies to produce super-hot pods, but you can still produce extremely good yields.

If you are in an area, whether too cold or too dry, where it is difficult to grow chillies, then growing them hydroponically is an ideal solution. These days you can pick up relatively cheap solutions that are easy to manage and do not take up too much space. It is certainly something to consider and is a very good way of growing the hotter, more temperamental chillies at home.

ORNAMENTAL CHILLI VARIETIES

As well as the edible varieties of chillies that we have been talking about up until now, there are ornamental pepper varieties. These don't produce awe-inspiring flowers or tasty fruits, in fact, in many cases the fruit is inedible, though some of the edible cultivars produce a beautiful display. However, they love the summer heat, and the fruits are usually very prolific and colourful. They are great in borders and beds to add a splash of exotic colour.

The fruits come in a wide range of colours from white, purple and lavender through to the more usual red, orange or yellow. As the fruits ripen, so they change colour, with the exact colours depending on the variety of ornamental chilli planted. Some varieties have variegated foliage, making them even more attractive in your border. As both large and small cultivars are available, you can find a plant that is ideal for any spot in your garden.

Ornamental chillies love a warm, sunny spot in your garden. These do well in full sun or partial shade, though in the former situation, the fruits don't tend to have as much colour or be as abundant.

Chillies like a moist, well-drained soil that has a lot of organic material in it, is. If you are planting them outside rather than in containers, dig in a lot of compost when you plant them, so they have the best growing environment. Chillies are greedy plants, even the ornamental varieties, so feed them regularly.

There is no need to prune ornamental chilli plants, but you can pinch out the growing tips if you want them to keep their shape or remain compact.

Of course, if you are growing ornamental chillies outside, you need to ensure they have the right type of climate. Ornamental varieties require the same climate conditions as their edible counterparts. Although some varieties are not edible, others, such as Little Elf, can be eaten. Always check the packet when you buy the seeds and do not try to eat any that say they are inedible.

Other ornamental varieties such as *Solanum pseudocapsicum*, also known as *Solanum capiscastrum*, are known as the false capsicum and are members of the tomato family. There are a lot of members of the tomato family that are toxic to humans and animals, including the popular ornamental chilli, Winter Cherry. This is very toxic to humans and should not be consumed. If you own a dog, it is better not to grow this variety as it is toxic to pets when eaten. The Winter Cherry variety is often sold around Christmas time and usually right next to the edible varieties, just to confuse matters. Make sure you check the labels very carefully as you don't want to risk mixing them up.

Some of the popular ornamental chilli varieties include:

- Numex Twilight – an edible variety that produces a lovely display. It has dark green leaves that contrasts well with the abundance of purple flowers. The fruits grow to about ¾"/2cm, tapering towards the end, maturing through yellow to orange and finally red. You often see all the colours on the plant at the same time, making it very attractive. The plant grows to about 18"/45cm in height and has the advantage of being very drought resistant.

- Etna – named for the eruption of bright red chillies it produces, this is a newer variety bred in Italy. It is another edible chilli variety that is grown ornamentally and is very hot, coming in at around 65,000 Scovilles. The plants grow to a medium size and produce a good crop of chillies that grow in bunches.
- Paper Lantern – this is a lovely ornamental chilli variety that has bushy growth and produces abundant clusters of emerald green, teardrop-shaped chilli pods. As the pods mature, the colour turns to a blood red. Although this is a very pretty looking chilli, it is one of the hottest you can lay your hands on at around 450,000 Scoville heat units. This chilli variety will grow happily in containers or a sheltered border.
- Patio Fire – a dwarf chilli variety that is content in a container, growing to around 12cm/6 inches high and about 30cm/one foot wide. It produces lots of very small leaves and attractive, ½" fruits that change colour from cream to orange to dark red as they mature. Although small, these chillies pack a punch and mature in around 80 days, meaning they are colourful throughout the summer months. This is a prolific fruiter, with each plant producing hundreds of small pods.
- Bolivian Rainbow – a very colourful plant, producing fruits that range in colour from yellow to orange, to red and purple. This is a very easy chilli to grow and does well in containers, limiting their growth to a manageable size.
- Filius Blue – a lovely chilli with foliage tinged with purple and, in some cases, slightly speckled with white spots. The plants grow to about two feet tall and have a short growing season, so are ideal outside of the usual sub-tropical growing environment. The chilli pods are very small and egg-shaped. Initially, they are a purple/blue colour, which they retain until they ripen to a pleasant shade of red. Unlike most other chillies, this variety becomes cooler as it matures, but the immature chillies rate between 20,000 and 30,000 on the Scoville heat scale.
- Royal Black – this chilli is lovely to grow in your back garden, being tall and bushy, with dark purple leaves, occasionally tipped with white or green. The pods are shaped like bullets and are hot. They start out dark purple and ripen to a bright red colour.
- Numex Centennial – bred specifically for containers, this is a very attractive ornamental variety with purple-veined leaves. The fruits

are gorgeous, standing upright and ripening from purple to orange, yellow and then red. A good looking chilli originally bred for the centennial celebrations of New Mexico University.

There are many more varieties of chilli that can be grown ornamentally, though these are some of the most popular and commonly grown. Almost any type of chilli can be grown as an ornamental plant, but if you can eat the chillies too, then that is a bonus. Chillies make for an excellent addition to a border or flower bed where they add some colour that changes throughout the growing season, providing you can grow chillies outdoors where you live.

PESTS, DISEASES, AND PROBLEMS

Every plant suffers from a variety of pests, diseases, and other problems. Depending on where in the world you are living and how you are growing your chillies you may encounter some, none or many of these problems. I have detailed many of the problems facing chilli growers, but a lot of these issues are only found in very specific geographic areas. I want you to understand all of the potential pests and diseases so you can take action as quickly as possible if you spot a problem. One of the biggest pests I face, for example, are my cats, which for some odd reason have developed a taste for chilli leaves.

Keeping a close eye on your chilli plants will help you to spot any problems before they become serious. If you spot a problem early on and take action, you have more chance of stopping the problem before it causes irrevocable damage to your plant and spreads to other plants you are growing.

Growing indoors, hydroponically and in a greenhouse will reduce the number of problems you have with your plants. One of the keys to reducing pest and disease problems is to ensure there is sufficient space between the plants for the air to circulate. This prevents many of the more commonly found problems and is something many of us forget as we cram our plants together.

Water your chilli plants from below if you are growing in pots as chillies prefer being watered this way and, unless you are specifically giving your plants a foliar spray, avoid getting water on the leaves. Overwatering causes a lot of problems with chillies, so be careful not to water them too much.

Diagnosing Problems

When you first encounter a problem, you need to diagnose it and understand exactly what is causing the problem so you can treat it appropriately. This section is designed to help you determine what a problem is based on the symptoms the plant is exhibiting. In the following sections, the individual pests and diseases will be discussed in more detail, together with appropriate treatments.

Leaf Problems

- Yellowing – aphids, whitefly, *Verticillium* wilt, nematodes or mineral deficiency. Can also be caused by overwatering
- Browning – too much nitrogen in the soil or plant food, *Phytophthora* blight or bacterial leaf spot
- Curling – usually caused by pests such as spider mites, thrips or aphids, though some viruses cause leaf curl
- Holes – caterpillars, flea beetles, slugs or snails, though sometimes caused by mineral deficiencies
- Scorching – scalding from the sun or burns from chemicals or fertiliser
- Spots and Blotches – powdery mildew, bacterial leaf spot, *Cercospora* leaf spot, *Phytophthora* blight, viruses or sometimes from the use of chemicals

Plant Problems

- Browning Stems – too little water, *Phytophthora* blight or bacterial leaf spot
- Wilting – too much or too little water, *Phytophthora* blight, bacterial wilt or *Verticillium* wilt
- Plants Falling Over – usually damping off, poorly supported plant, weak root system or waterlogged soil
- Slow Growth – poor quality soil, temperature too cool, not enough light, though some chilli varieties are just very slow to grow
- Poor Germination – old or non-viable seeds, temperature too low, compost too moist so seeds have rotten

Chilli plant, leaves drooping due to lack of water

Chilli Pod Problems

- Holes – pepper maggots, slugs or snails, though can be caused by animals or birds
- Spots and Discolouration – grey mold, thrips, *Phytophthora* blight, bacterial soft rot, Anthracnose, bacterial leaf spot or mineral deficiency
- Distortion – viruses, spider mites, thrips or poor pollination
- Flower Drop or No Chillies Produced – poor pollination or unexpected temperature drop during growing season
- Soft Rot – grey mold, bacterial soft rot
- Failure to Ripen – growing season too short, not enough light or temperatures too cool

In the next sections, we talk in more detail about the pests, diseases, and problems that chilli plants can face. Remember, the quicker you take action when you spot a problem, the less chance that the plant will be permanently damaged and the problem spreads to the rest of your plants.

Common Chilli Pests

There are a lot of different pests that are more than happy to munch on your valuable chilli plants, from deer, rabbits, raccoons and other rodents through to your pets. My cats frequently chew on my chilli plants or sit in the pots and are the biggest problem I have, though for you it may be different.

The two main types of problem that face your plant are living agents and non-living agents. Non-living agents include environmental factors such as too much or too little water, insufficient light, poor nutrition, low temperature, air pollution or poor soil pH. Living agents are typically fungi, viruses, insects, and bacteria.

Insect Pests

There are a lot of insects that can affect your chilli plants. Which ones you will encounter depends on where you live in the world and where you are growing your plants. In most cases, you won't have any problems with your chilli plants, but you need to be aware of potential problems so you can spot and resolve them should your plants be affected in any way.

Slugs and Snails

These are most of our worst nightmares. They will devour your chilli seedlings overnight, leaving useless stumps behind. These are very easy to diagnose as you can see the slime trails left behind. Slugs are hermaphrodites and produce dozens of eggs, several times a year, quickly spreading all over your garden. The egg clusters are white jelly or tiny round eggs and should be destroyed as soon as you see them.

The best way to control these pests is to patrol your garden every dusk and dawn. Find any slugs and snails, use a torch to help you spot them, and collect them in a bucket. Then either dispose of them a long way away from your precious plants or destroy them. They can be found wedged into crevices in your greenhouse, on the inside of pots or even on the underside of pots. They are very craft and excellent at hiding.

Keep your growing area clear of debris and rubbish as this minimises hiding places for these pests. Slug pellets are an option, but they are harmful to beneficial animals such as hedgehogs and can harm anything that eats slugs or snails. There are plenty of things you can use that supposedly stop slugs, such as copper tape, crushed eggshells, coffee grounds and so on, but these don't work effectively or consistently. Beer traps do work, though make sure you change them regularly as they smell horrible after a while. Thorny brambles are very effective at stopping slugs, but they need to be placed quite thickly around your plants.

The most effective way to get rid of slugs is to remove them by hand. Keep doing that, and you will get the population under control and protect your plants.

Aphids

This pest is very hard to spot until the infestation has become serious because they hide under the leaves and are green in colour. They usually gather on the young shoots where they suck the sap from the plants, causing leaf curl and distortion. Chillies grown indoors tend to get the worst aphid infestations because they are isolated from natural predators. When watering your plants, check the new growth and the underside of the leaves for signs of aphid infestation.

Growing chillies in a greenhouse or polytunnel makes it easier to control aphids as you can release ladybirds and ladybird larvae into the greenhouse, which will eat these pests.

Aphids can be removed by rubbing them off between your fingers, making sure not to damage the leaves. This works in smaller infestations, but with more serious cases, this can be very difficult to do effectively.

Sprays can be used, though make sure that any chemical spray used is safe for food crops. Diluting a teaspoon of dish soap in two litres of water produces an effective aphid control spray. Use this on the underside of the leaves to kill off these pests. Neem oil is another good natural pesticide. Just remember that pesticides are not selective and will kill pests and beneficial insects alike.

Regularly check your plants for aphids, making sure to inspect the underside of the leaves. If the infestation is minimal, pick the aphids off by hand to prevent them from spreading.

Caterpillars
These don't usually affect chilli plants, preferring tastier and easier to eat plants. You may spot dark eggs, a millimeter or two across, on the underside of the leaves or find rolled up leaves with caterpillars inside. These are pretty easy to spot, and both eggs and adults can easily be removed by hand. Hotter varieties are not normally affected by caterpillars as they can't bear the heat either/

Flea Beetles
These pests affect a lot of different plants, including chillies. Flea beetles are about 2mm long, shiny and have long back legs, which allows them to jump. The adults feed on the underside of the leaves, which results in either irregularly shaped holes or small pits in the leaves. The larvae burrow into the soil where they feed on the roots, but usually cause very little damage.

This pest is avoiding by germinating, growing and potting on your seedlings rapidly, which gets them past the stage where they are vulnerable to the damage caused by this beetle. Growing in a sterile soil prevents flea beetle infestations and ensures it takes longer for them to get established, if at all.

Flea beetles do not like water and can be discouraged by spraying your plants with water during the day, though be careful to avoid scorching the leaves. This is when they feed and are active, which means the water repels them from the plants. Alternatively, put some rubber gloves on and pick the beetles off by hand.

Pepper Maggots
These are about half an inch long as an adult, pointed at the head end and a white/yellow colour. They feed on the core of the chilli pods, making them turn red too early and rot from the inside. Check the pods on the plants for tiny entry holes and, if you find any, remove and destroy the infected chillies. If the pods are left on the plant to rot, then they will attract other pests.

Nematodes (root knot)

These are very small, transparent roundworms that reside in the soil, feeding on the roots of your plants. This root damage hinders the chilli plant from taking up nutrients and water. Depending on the severity of the infestation, symptoms may include wilting, lack of fruit and knots on the root which can be as large as a pea.

Nematodes are more prevalent in sandy soils rather than clay soils. Improving the soil with organic matter and rotating your crops helps reduce the incidences of nematodes. Growing in containers usually eliminates the risk of nematodes, but you may still encounter them. If you do, then re-pot the chilli, removing as much soil as possible from the plant before putting it in the new pot. Some varieties of chilli are particularly susceptible to nematodes, while other varieties have developed resistance to these pests.

Spider Mites

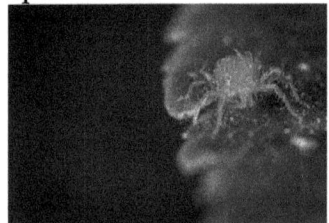

These can become a serious problem and cause a lot of damage to your plants, particularly when the weather is hot and dry. Like many other pests, they feed on the underside of the leaves and will appear to be tiny, moving red dots. In serious infestations you will see webs on the plant too. Left uncontrolled, these will kill your plants.

In the early stages of infestation, infected leaves will begin to turn downwards and take on a speckled appearance. The easiest way to identify a spider mite infestation is to hold a piece of white paper under a leaf which you suspect is infected and tap the leaf a few times. You should then see some movement as the mites fall on to the paper.

Increasing the humidity reduces the reproduction rate of the mites. Spray infected leaves with water or move the plant into a more humid room, such as a bathroom. There are chemical sprays that combat spider mites, but you need to make sure that they can be used safely on food crops.

Thrips

These pests are very small and slim, and are black, yellow, white or brown in colour. Infected leaves distort and curl upwards, and the underside of the leaves develop a silvery sheen that turns bronze over time. The pods will also be damaged, which appears as brown or silver marks. Removing affected leaves and pods by hand is a good way to control these, though there are chemical sprays available.

Whitefly
These are particularly irritating pests and form a cloud when you disturb a plant. They are about 1½mm long and have broad wings. They suck the juices from the leaves, so they shrivel, turn yellow and drop off. As well as this, whiteflies secrete honeydew that coats the leaves making them sticky and covered in black, sooty mould.

Controlling whiteflies is quite difficult as they are only vulnerable to chemicals in the final stage of their lifecycle while flying. They reproduce rapidly, so require spraying frequently, which can damage your plant. Removing the flies and leaves by hand helps, as does a spray made up of diluted dish soap. It can take several weeks to completely eradicate an infestation of whiteflies. Wrapping sticky tape around your hand with the sticky side out and brushing against the infected plants will capture some whiteflies and help reduce the infestation.

Common Chilli Diseases

Chillies suffer from their fair share of diseases, and again, regular inspection and rapid treatment is the best way to prevent any disease from taking hold and destroying your crop. Plants grown indoors or in a greenhouse tend to suffer from fewer diseases, though ensure there is sufficient space between the plants for air circulation to prevent fungal diseases from taking hold and spreading. As you read this section, you will see that most diseases are either caused by infected seeds or from damp conditions.

Anthracnose
This fungal infection is more common when there is high humidity, high temperatures and insufficient plant spacing. The pods will still grow, but this disease damages them with sunken, round spots that can be as big as an inch across. When the environment is particularly moist, you may even see yellow or pink spore masses growing on the plant.

Combat this disease by ensuring there is sufficient space between your plants, using disease-free seeds and through crop rotation. Should this disease develop on your chilli plants, remove and destroy any infected pods. In serious infections, you may need to use a fungicide spray.

Bacterial Leaf Spot
The bacterium that causes this in chillies also causes bacterial spot in tomatoes, so make sure the two types of plants are not planted close together. The disease develops in moist environments but usually comes from infected seeds.

The first symptom of this disease is small, water sacked areas of up to a quarter of an inch across on the leaves. As the disease develops, the spots develop black centres with yellow halos around the outside. On the underside of the leaf, the spot is raised while on the top side, it will be depressed. Severely infected leaves yellow and fall off the plant, resulting in pods that are exposed to sun scald.

Buying disease-free seeds is the best way to avoid this disease. Copper-based fungicides have some success in controlling this disease, though often cause growth issues with the plant.

Bacterial Soft Rot
This bacterium affects the pods of your plants, softening the internal tissue before turning the pod into a foul-smelling, watery mass. In wet conditions, this disease becomes worse because the bacteria get splashed from the ground onto the chilli pods. Insects also spread this disease.

Control this disease by keeping plants off the ground or growing indoors, where rain cannot spread the spores. Controlling insects can help slow or stop the spread of this disease. Infected pods should be immediately removed and destroyed.

Bacterial Wilt
The early symptoms of this disease are wilting leaves, which means it is often confused with lack of water. Push your finger into the soil up to the first knuckle to check how dry the soil is before watering more as overwatering causes further problems. After a few days, the whole plants wilts and the plant dies.

It is possible to test for infection by cutting some roots and lower stems, suspending them in water and looking for milky white streams coming off them.

Unfortunately, there isn't any treatment for an infected plant. Should you find any plants with this disease, immediately isolate and destroy them. Buying seeds from reputable dealers can help avoid this disease.

***Cercospora* Leaf Spot (Frog Eye)**
This fungal infection is worst in long spells of warm, wet weather. The symptoms of the disease are small, brown, round lesions on the leaves that are watery in appearance. In more serious infections, there will be leaf drop.

Minimise this problem by ensuring there is sufficient spacing between the plants for air circulation. In severe infections, you can use a fungicide, but use food safe chemicals otherwise you risk ingesting them when eating the chillies.

Damping Off Disease

There are several potential causes of this disease, including poor seed quality, not planting the seeds deep enough, too much salt in the soil, nutrient deficiencies and the seed trays being too wet.

The seeds may fail to emerge from the soil, known as pre-emergence damping off, or may collapse when small, known as post-emergence damping off. In some cases, the seedlings are stunted, known as collar rot or root rot.

One of the most common causes of this disease is poorly drained soil. Ensuring good air circulation around the seedlings can also help reduce the incidences of this disease. It can be treated with a copper-based fungicide or a chamomile tea mixture. Adding some sand, perlite or vermiculite to the potting compost will help it to drain better and hopefully avoid this disease.

Grey Mould

This is quite common in chilli plants, being caused by the *Botrytis cinerea* fungus. The most common symptom is a sudden collapse of young leaves, flowers, and stems. On the dead plant matter, you will see grey spore masses that are powdery, like ashes (*cinerea* is Latin for ashy).

High humidity and poor air circulation make this disease worse, so ensure the air can circulate around the plants. Remove and destroy any infected areas immediately and, in serious infections, look at using a fungicide.

***Phytophthora* Blight (Chilli Wilt)**

This is a water-borne fungus, commonly found in wet and waterlogged areas. It affects all parts of the plant, causing symptoms similar to those of fruit rot, root rot, and leaf blight. Infected plants will wilt and die in a matter of days. Unfortunately, once the fungus reaches the roots, the plant cannot be saved.

You may find that just a part of the plant is infected, rather than the whole plant, usually bordered with white mould. If this is the case, remove and destroy the infected part and surrounding plant material immediately.

Ensure the soil has good drainage and avoid over watering your plants. The fruit rot and leaf blight can be treated using a fungicide, though the root rot is typically terminal.

Powdery Mildew
This usually affects the leaves and is most common in warm, wet conditions. Powdery mildew is more common on older leaves and will appear as white, powdery growth which can grow, so it covers the whole underside of the leaf.

Diseased leaves will drop, exposing the pods to sun scald. Remove any infected areas immediately and treat with a fungicide. Incidences of this disease can be minimised by ensuring there is sufficient air circulation around the plants and avoiding getting water on the leaves.

Verticillium Wilt
This is caused by the soil-borne fungus, *Verticillium dahliae* and can infect your plant at any time during its growth stage. Unlike many other diseases, this is more common when the air is cool, and the soil temperatures are low.

Infected plants will often have stunted growth, and the leaves will yellow. As the disease takes hold, there will be leaf drop, and the plant can even die. Cutting the stem will usually show a brown discolouration. The only control for this disease is good crop rotation practices.

White Mould
This fungal disease causes blight and rot on any part of the plant, above or below the soil. Initially, the infected area will take on a greasy, dark green, waterlogged appearance. The stems develop lesions which are grey to brown in colour.

Control this disease with good spacing between plants, crop rotation, and good soil drainage. Any infected plants or plant material should be immediately removed and destroyed.

Viral Diseases

These are some of the potential viral diseases that can affect your chilli plants. Viruses tend to be harder to control and treat, but are less common. Buying certified disease-free seeds is one of the best ways to avoid viral diseases.

Pepper Mottle Virus (PeMV) and Pepper Mosaic Virus
This is caused when infected insects, commonly aphids, come in contact with your plants. Symptoms include distorted fruit, poor pod yield, and stunted growth. Control of the virus is difficult. Remove any infected plants and control the aphid population on surrounding plants.

Tobacco Etch Virus (TEV)
Another virus spread by infected insects, usually aphids. Symptoms include stunted growth, distorted leaves, and dark green leaf veins. Remove infected plants, control aphids and, if this disease is common in your area, use resistant chilli varieties.

Tobacco Mosaic Virus (TMV)
A very infectious disease that is difficult to get rid of once it has infected your plants. It is carried by infected tobacco in cigarettes and spreads after smoking or handling tobacco. Symptoms are mottled fruit, stunted growth, curling leaves and excessive leaf drop.

If you smoke, wash your hands in milk, which kills this virus, before handling your chilli plants. Control of this virus is difficult. Remove any infected plants immediately to prevent the virus from spreading.

Common Chilli Problems

With good air circulation and watering practices, you can avoid many of the common problems that affect chillies. However, the other frequent cause of problems is nutrient or mineral deficiency. These are more common in container grown chillies than in soil grown plants, but a good feeding schedule with a quality plant food will prevent most of these problems. Always read the instructions of your plant food and apply the appropriate quantity at the correct dilution.

There are plant foods specifically formulated for chilli plants, though a good quality tomato or seaweed fertiliser will be suitable for your plants. Be careful not to overfeed your plants as that can cause more harm than good.

Here are some of the common mineral deficiencies and their symptoms:

- Calcium – new leaves will be stunted or misshapen. Existing leaves are unaffected, remaining green
- Iron – young leaves turn a yellow or white colour with green veins while existing leaves are unaffected
- Nitrogen – leaves at the top of the plant are light green, but lower leaves are yellow, and the bottom leaves also shrivelled
- Potassium – younger leaves yellow at the tips and edges with dead and yellow patches developing on some leaves
- Carbon Dioxide – stunted growth with white spots on some leaves
- Manganese – yellow spots and/or elongated holes appearing between veins

- Phosphate – darker than normal leaves and leaf drop
- Magnesium – the lower leaves turn yellow from the outside in with the veins remaining green.

These are the most obvious symptoms of mineral deficiency, but if you are regularly feeding your plants, then you should have no issues with this. Liquid feeds are better as they can be more easily absorbed by your plants but do not overfeed or water as this will harm your plants.

Frequently Asked Questions

There are some common questions people ask when growing chillies, particularly when starting out. This chapter answers those questions and hopefully will help you get started on your quest of growing chillies at home.

Can chillies be grown outside?
Once the risk of frost has passed, they can be planted outdoors. However, depending on the length of your growing season there may not be enough time for the fruit to fully ripen. Hotter varieties require more warmth to produce fruit, which may not be possible where you live. The plants are also subject to the vagrancies of the weather, which can mean your chillies struggle if the growing season is poor. I'd recommend growing indoors or under glass unless you are in a tropical or sub-tropical area purely because the weather can be too variable for chillies to grow well.

Can chillies be grown in a conservatory or sunroom?
Yes, they can, it will act like a greenhouse, though be aware the plants need plenty of water as it can get hot in a conservatory. It is important to ensure there is sufficient air flow in your conservatory, which can be solved with a couple of open windows and a fan. In colder weather, you may need a heater to keep the conservatory warm enough and prevent the temperature dropping below that which chillies find acceptable.

Are there mild varieties of chillies I can grow?
There are many different mild varieties of chilli. One of my favourites is Hungarian Black, which has a lot of flavour but is still quite mild.

Why are the flowers falling off of my plants?
This is quite common in chillies grown indoors or in a greenhouse. Chillies are self-pollinating, so do not require insects to produce fruit. However, sometimes the stamen does not touch the pistil and creates a sterile flower. An occasional shake of your plants will solve this problem. This can also happen when too little water stresses the plant and it gets too hot. When under stress, most plants will drop their flowers in an attempt to ensure their survival.

Why are leaves falling off my plants?
You may notice the lower leaves turn yellow or fall off, which is a sign that your plants are getting too much water. Keep the compost moist but not waterlogged. If you notice any leaves from the top of the plant dropping off, then this is usually because the plant isn't getting enough water or suffering from environmental shock such as re-potting or a change of environment.

When should I harvest the fruits?
This depends on the variety. Most can be harvested any time during their ripening stage. Some varieties will not fully mature outdoors anywhere other than a tropical or sub-tropical environment. Many varieties can be picked and used while they are still green. Harvesting the fruit usually encourages the plant to produce even more, hence some growers will remove some of the fruit early in the growing season before it is mature for a larger crop.

How do I stop my chillies growing too big?
Pinch off the growing stem when it reaches about around 30cm/12" in height. This forces the plant to bush out rather than grow tall and leggy.

Where Should I Buy My Seeds From?
I would always recommend buying your seeds from reputable suppliers. I regularly see people wondering what plants they are growing because they have bought seeds online from disreputable suppliers who provide them with the wrong seeds. All the big seed companies stock the hottest and most popular chilli varieties plus you can contact specialist chilli suppliers who will provide you with the rarer cultivars. By buying from reputable suppliers, you know you are getting good quality seeds that will have a high germination rate and are disease free. If you have any problems, the reputable seed companies are always happy to help resolve those issues however they can.

How Can I Help My Seeds Germinate?
There are a few things you can do which may help your seeds germinate. Firstly, try warming the compost you are using to just above room temperature. Chillies are from a hot climate and need the soil to be warm.

Try soaking the seeds overnight in warm water or a weak cup of tea as this helps soften the shell and can improve the germination rate, just don't leave them in their too long. Avoid overwatering during the germination phase, keep the soil damp, but not wet and you will have more seedlings appear.

Breeding Your Own Chilli Varieties

Once you have grown chillies a few times and become hooked, you may want to have a go at creating your own varieties. Whether you want to try to breed your own super-hot chilli or just a milder variety is entirely up to you. This is how Ed Currie created the Carolina Reaper, by cross-breeding hot chilli varieties.

Chilli peppers contain two sets of chromosomes, and the flowers contain both the male and female parts, so they are self-fertile. When a chilli plant self-pollinates, it creates seeds that will produce a plant very similar to the parent plant.

However, chillies are cross-fertile, which means one variety of chilli can pollinate another variety, which is how new cultivars are born. This can happen deliberately, or it can happen by accident as pollinating insects carry pollen from one variety to another. This is a reason why sometimes you will find a chilli plant having the 'wrong' type of chilli on, because it has cross-pollinated with another variety.

If you are planning on creating a new variety, then you need to isolate both parent plants and ensure that accidental pollination cannot happen otherwise you cannot guarantee what the result will be. While you are building the seed stock, the plants also need isolating to ensure no cross-pollination can occur.

There are over three and a half thousand different varieties of capsicum in the world, with more being developed every year as people cross breed chillies in search of new strains. You may cross breed to introduce disease resistance, create hotter chillies, larger chillies, sweeter chillies, or any number of reasons.

To create a new cultivar, you need to start with one parent that is a stable variety, i.e., the seeds produce new plants virtually identical to the parent.

This plant is then isolated, and pollen from a different variety is used to pollinate the flowers on the plant. Depending on how you want to approach this, you can leave a single flower on the plant and pollinate it with a donor plant, or you can pollinate all of the flowers on the plant. The latter will result in more varieties whereas the first approach will result in seeds that are more likely to produce consistent results.

Say you crossed a purple, small podded chilli plant with an orange, long-podded one. The resulting plants may have long, short or mid-sized pods, and could be any colour from purple through to orange. If the plant looks similar to the mother plant, don't worry as the seeds in the new pod contain chromosomes from both parent plants.

These first generation seeds are known as F1 or first filial generation. These seeds will produce plants that are more or less identical. You will often see F1 varieties for sale as growers have crossed two varieties and know what the resulting plants will look like.

Growing F1 seeds produces relatively consistent results, but the fun comes when you grow the next generation, the F2 plants. These will have a lot more variety as recessive genes in the plants can become dominant. F1 pods are usually controlled by the dominant genes of the parent plants, but the more you breed the plants and the further you get from the F1 children, the more variety there will be in the traits of the plant.

Selling F2 or F3 seeds is harder because of the variation in plant characteristics. However, some growers want these sort of plants because of the genetic possibilities. Every now and again, a breeder will hit the jackpot and create a new variety that is stable and of interest.

To produce a new variety of chilli, you need to keep growing the plant for several years. Each year you choose the pods and plants that have the characteristic you are trying to breed. With each generation, there is more chance that the seeds will breed true as you filter out the undesirable genes, choosing only those that have the traits you want.

After around seven generations your plants are going to be over 99% true to the characteristics you have bred. The chromosomes have become virtually homozygous again, though there is still some chance for a genetic wildcard to be dealt. Breeding new varieties take time and patience and isn't for everyone.

If you want to produce better quality seeds that are more stable, then you need to start with more plants of each variety, rather than just the one plant we talked about in the examples above. If you started with ten, twenty or even fifty of each variety and cross-pollinated them; then you will end up with better quality of plants. Starting with just two limits the gene pool, which can result in weak or sickly plants several generations down the line.

It's the same with humans as they reproduce. If the gene pool is too small, then there is the chance of genetic abnormalities. In the Middle Ages in Europe, the royal families bred amongst themselves so as not to dilute the power base. Cousins and even siblings would marry, resulting in a weak gene pool that developed deformities and illnesses such as hemophilia, known as the Royal disease.

The same applies to your chilli plants. If they don't have enough variation in the gene pool, from having multiple plants of the same, true varieties at the start of the process, there is the chance that genetic abnormalities can appear.

There are forums and groups online dedicated to cross breeding chillies. It's fun to do but requires a lot of time to pollinate the plants, keep the records and so on. It can take years before you have a new, stable variety during which you need a lot of space to grow the plants. Because of the need to isolate the plants from pollinators, you have to have sealed greenhouses or polytunnels to work in, though you can work with the small plastic greenhouses many of us use at home. However, if you have space, time and patience, then you could pursue the dream of creating the world's hottest chilli pepper.

Chapter 3

Preserving & Cooking Chilies

MAKING CHILLI SAUCES

One of the most popular uses for chillies, particularly the very hot ones is to create a chilli sauce. You can make your chilli sauce as hot or as mild as you want. Of course, people who grow the seriously hot chillies like to make the hottest sauces possible, which you can do.

The heat and taste of a sauce depend greatly on the type of chilli you are using. Peppers such as the habanero varieties add a fruity flavour, rounding out the sauce and giving it greater depth. A chilli such as the Carolina Reaper basically just burns its way through your digestive tract when you make a sauce with it. Part of the fun is experimenting with the different types of chilli and combining different varieties to make a great tasting sauce.

Please remember when handing the hot chillies, even the milder varieties, that they will have a burning effect on sensitive areas, particularly the eyes and nose. I strongly recommend wearing kitchen gloves, latex are best and being extremely careful not to touch your eyes, mouth or face. Once finished, carefully remove the gloves and wash your hands thoroughly. Trust me; you'll only touch something sensitive once after handling chillies, the pain will make sure you never do it again.

Making chilli sauces is certainly an art form and here is a fairly generic recipe that is made with any chilli varieties you have. There are plenty of other recipes online, including some designed to burn like crazy, it depends entirely on the type or mix of chillies used. This is a simple recipe that does not take very long to make and is easily tailored to your personal preferences.

Ingredients:
- 30-50g/1 cup chillies
- 7oz/200g diced tomatoes (canned or fresh)
- 50g/¼ cup granulated (white) sugar
- 60ml/¼ cup white wine vinegar
- Salt to taste

Method:
1. Put all the ingredients into a saucepan and heat on a high heat until boiling
2. Reduce the heat to medium
3. Simmer for 7-10 minutes until the sauce thickens a little, stirring regularly
4. Remove from the heat and leave to stand for 5 minutes
5. Put the mixture through a food processor, in batches if necessary, and process until smooth
6. Jar or can for storage

That is a very simple recipe for a chilli sauce, but there are many more you can try. In any of the following recipes, you can swap out the chillies mentioned in the recipe with any that you have to hand.

Fermenting Chillies

Many chilli sauce recipes call for the chillies to be fermented first, a process that can take a couple of weeks. This releases more flavour and helps make for a better tasting hot sauce. Tabasco sauce, for example, is made from fermented chillies, as are many of the other commercially available sauces.

This fermented mash is essentially chillies mashed with salt, then aged until they have broken down. It is important that you understand you are not making anything alcoholic here or rotting the chillies. This fermentation is designed to preserve the chillies and create a deeper flavour. When you create a mash, you will know very quickly if it has gone wrong because it will smell rotten and off. There is a very definite smell to fermenting chillies, and you will quickly learn when it is done incorrectly.

Making Your Chilli Mash
A chilli mash can be made from any type of chilli, even ones you have dried. You just need to consider how thick the walls are. Chillies with thicker walls may need to be strained after fermentation is complete to remove the coarse skin. Thinner walled chillies do not need straining and are usually deseeded first (if at all), so you have a smoother mash later on.

Start by chopping the chilli peppers. This can be done by hand, in a mortar and pestle or, most commonly, in a food processor.

Put the chopped chillies in a bowl and add salt at a ratio of one teaspoon of salt to each pound of chopped chillies. Avoid table salt as this contains additives. Sea salt or Kosher salt is the best to use as there are no additives in these salts.

Mix the salt into the chillies, then transfer to a jar. Press the mixture down to remove air pockets, leaving about an inch headspace between the top of your chilli mash and the top of the jar. A liquid brine will form in the jar, and it will rise to cover the chillies. Make sure the chillies remain covered by the brine once it has formed as this will stop the chillies from rotting.

Alternatively, you can make a brine to pour over your chillies. Mix three tablespoons of sea salt with a quart (950ml/2¼ pints) of unchlorinated water and pour this into the jar over the peppers.

Screw the lid onto the jar and then put it somewhere out of direct sunlight while it ferments. The ideal temperature is between 13-24°C/55-75°F. Leave the mash to ferment for a couple of weeks. Every two or three days, you must 'burp' the jars by removing the lid to release the built-up gases.

After a week or two, the mash is ready and can be used to make a chilli sauce, or stored in your refrigerator where it will last for at least a year.

If you feel your mash is a little bitter, add some lime juice, vinegar, sugar or honey which should take away the bitter edge that can sometimes happen.

Chilli Sauce Recipes

There are a huge variety of chilli sauce recipes, and almost every chilli grower will have their favourite recipe. Here are some of my favourite recipes that you can make with your chillies, whether home-grown or store bought. Feel free to adjust the recipes and experiment with them, tailoring them to your particular tastes and to what you have at hand.

Peachy Scotch Bonnet Sauce

This is a great recipe, with the combination of sweet from the peaches and heat from the chillies making for a surprisingly tasty and versatile sauce. It can be used for anything, though it is particularly good with both fish and chicken.

Ingredients:
- 454g/1lb tomatoes (chopped)
- 170g/6oz Scotch Bonnet chilli peppers (chopped)
- 2 garlic cloves (chopped)
- 1 peach (peeled, pitted and chopped)
- 60ml/¼ cup apple cider vinegar
- 2 tablespoons honey
- 1 tablespoon English mustard powder
- 1 teaspoon salt
- ½ teaspoon black pepper powder
- ½ teaspoon dried cardamom

Method:
1. Ferment the chillies, garlic, peach, and tomato in a brine solution for a couple of weeks, following the instructions given previously
2. Once fermentation has finished, put the contents of the jar into a saucepan along with the rest of the ingredients and bring to the boil
3. Reduce the heat and simmer, occasionally stirring, for 15 minutes
4. Remove from heat and allow to cool
5. Process in your food processor until smooth
6. Pour into sterilised jars, seal and refrigerate
7. Leave for one to two weeks to mature before using

Habanero and Mango Hot Sauce

A great hot sauce, again, offsetting the sweet and fiery tastes to make a delicious sauce that has many uses. Try using a variety of different habanero peppers for a well-rounded, fruity sauce that makes your eyes water.

Ingredients:
- 4 garlic cloves (chopped)
- 2 small mangos (peeled and chopped)
- 2 serrano chilli peppers (chopped)
- 2 medium tomatoes (chopped)
- 1 habanero chilli pepper (chopped)
- 1 jalapeño chilli pepper (chopped)
- 1 small sweet onion (chopped)
- Juice of 1 lime
- 120ml/½ cup red wine vinegar (reduce the quantity for a thinner sauce)
- 60ml/¼ cup chopped cilantro (coriander)
- Salt and pepper to taste

Method:
1. Put everything into your food processor, pulsing until chopped, but not pureed
2. Pour everything into a saucepan and bring to the boil
3. Reduce the heat and simmer for a further 20 minutes
4. Thin the sauce, if required, by adding more vinegar, a few tablespoons at a time, and stirring well
5. Remove from the heat and then strain, if you prefer, or leave as is
6. Store in airtight jars and refrigerate
7. Leave for a couple of weeks for the flavours to mature before use

Honey Roast Hot Sauce

A great combination of hot and sweet that is used on almost any dish. Use whatever chilli peppers you have to hand or any combination of peppers to give a rounded taste.

Ingredients:
- 227g/8oz chilli peppers (chopped)
- 5 garlic cloves (chopped)
- 360ml/1½ cups apple cider vinegar
- 60ml/¼ cup honey
- 3 tablespoons dark rum
- 2 tablespoons brown sugar
- 2 tablespoons basil (freshly chopped)
- Juice of 1 lime
- Salt to taste

Method:
1. In a large bowl, mix the chillies, rum, honey, garlic, brown sugar, and basil, stirring well until thoroughly combined
2. Spread this mixture out on a large baking sheet, keeping the liquid that was in the bowl to one side
3. Preheat your oven to 180°C/350°F and roast for 10-12 minutes
4. Remove from the oven and allow to cool slightly
5. Add the mixture, together with the reserved liquid, to your food processor
6. Also add the apple cider vinegar and salt, to taste
7. Process until smooth
8. Add the lime juice by swirling it in across the liquid, then pour it into a storage container (bottle or jar)
9. Leave for 24-48 hours for the flavours to mature before use

Sweet Garlic Hot Sauce

A great sauce for a garlic lover that you can make as hot and fiery as you like. Although you can make this with sweet peppers, so the focus is on the garlic, there is nothing to stop you from throwing in hot peppers instead. A habanero or jalapeño will give this sauce a surprising kick. A great, general purpose sauce.

Ingredients:
- 57g/2oz sweet peppers (chopped)
- 6 garlic cloves (chopped)
- 160ml/⅔ cup white wine vinegar
- 1 teaspoon salt
- 1 teaspoon honey

Method:
1. Put all the ingredients into a saucepan and simmer for 15 minutes to soften
2. Remove from the heat and cool
3. Transfer to your food processor and process until smooth
4. Strain out the solids and then pour into a bottle
5. Store in the refrigerator

Searing Hot Serrano Sauce

This is a very tasty hot sauce that has an interesting combination of flavours and will make your eyes water.

Ingredients:
- 454g/1lb serrano peppers (finely chopped)
- 90ml/3oz white wine vinegar
- 45ml/1½oz reposado tequila
- 950ml/1-quart unchlorinated water
- 3 garlic cloves (minced)
- 3 tablespoons sea salt
- Juice of 1 lime

Method:
1. Ferment the chilli peppers for a week using the unchlorinated water and 3 tablespoons of sea salt
2. Pour the fermented peppers, including the brine, into a saucepan
3. Add the vinegar, tequila, and garlic, stirring well
4. Bring to a rapid boil, then reduce the heat and simmer for 15 minutes
5. Remove from the heat and leave to cool slightly
6. Add the mixture to your food processor together with the lime juice
7. Process until smooth
8. Strain to remove the solids, then bottle

Garlic Chilli Sauce

This is a good, general purpose sauce that is easy to make and can be used in almost any dish.

Ingredients:
- 114g/4oz chilli peppers (use any type to give your sauce the heat level you want)
- 4 garlic cloves (chopped)
- 2 tablespoons white vinegar
- 1 tablespoon granulated (white) sugar

Method:
1. Put everything into your food processor and blend until smooth
2. Pour the mixture into a saucepan and simmer for 10 minutes
3. Cool and season with salt and pepper to taste
4. Pour into a jar and store in your refrigerator

African Hot Sauce

This recipe calls for hot chilli peppers. Use any variety that you want to give the sauce the desired heat level. Red Sabina is a very good chilli for this sauce as it has both heat and flavour. Alternatively, any of the Habanero chilli peppers work well too.

Ingredients:
- 12 chilli peppers
- 2 garlic cloves
- 2 cans tomato paste
- 1 medium-sized onion
- 1 small green bell pepper
- 4 tablespoons malt (brown) vinegar
- 1 teaspoon granulated (white) sugar
- 1 teaspoon salt

Method:
1. Remove the stems and seeds from the chillies and bell pepper
2. Use a food processor or pestle and mortar to grind the bell pepper, garlic, onion and chilli peppers
3. Add all of the ingredients to a saucepan
4. Simmer for 1 to 2 hours, adding some cayenne pepper if required for extra taste
5. Cool, jar and store in your refrigerator

Harissa Hot Sauce

This taste is strongly associated with North African cuisine, particularly Tunisia. This sauce is great used by itself or can be mixed in with home-made sausages or burgers to give them a bit of a kick. This sauce does improve over time as the flavours mature and should be mixed well before use.

Ingredients:
- 40g/1 cup dried red chillies (use a hot variety)
- 10 garlic cloves
- ⅛ cup lemon juice
- 2 teaspoons ground cumin
- 2 teaspoons salt

Method:
1. Put the dried chillies into a saucepan and cover with water
2. Bring to the boil and simmer for 10 minutes

3. Remove from the heat and leave to stand for an hour
4. Drain the liquid from the chillies
5. Put the garlic, chillies, and salt into your food processor and puree
6. Add the lemon juice, blending after each addition, a little at a time until you get the desired consistency
7. Put the sauce into a sterilised jar and cover with extra-virgin olive oil
8. Seal the jar, shake well and refrigerate

Piri Piri Sauce

This sauce isn't the hottest on the market, but it is full of flavour and can be bought pre-made in stores. Use cayenne peppers to make this sauce or look for New Mexico or pequin chillies instead. For a hotter sauce, add some ground cayenne pepper or some red chilli flakes.

Ingredients:
- 4 chilli peppers (washed and chopped)
- 3 garlic cloves (minced)
- 4 tablespoons extra-virgin olive oil
- 1 tablespoon paprika
- 1 tablespoon fresh parsley (finely chopped)
- 1 teaspoon salt
- Juice of 1 lemon

Method:
1. Remove stems and seeds from the peppers, taking all the usual precautions
2. Process all the ingredients in a food processor until they form a paste
3. Fry for a few minutes
4. Store in your refrigerator and leave for a week for the flavour to develop

Thai Sweet Chilli Sauce

Thai sauces are very distinctive in their flavour and are usually quite heavy on the garlic. The best chillies to use are Bird's Eye and Serrano, which you can grow at home or you can find them in some stores, particularly in Asian markets.

Ingredients:
- 4 Serrano chillies (minced)
- 4 Bird's eye chillies (finely chopped)
- 200g/1 cup granulated (white) sugar
- 120ml/½ cup water

- 120ml/½ cup white vinegar (rice vinegar)
- 2 tablespoons garlic (finely minced)
- 1 tablespoon fresh lemon juice
- 1 tablespoon Thai fish sauce
- 1 teaspoon salt
- ½ teaspoon sweet paprika

Method:
1. Mix the sugar, water, vinegar, chillies, salt, paprika, and garlic together in a small saucepan
2. Over a medium heat, bring to a rolling boil and stir regularly to dissolve the solids
3. Reduce the heat to low and simmer, so the liquid reduces to a light syrup
4. Remove from the heat
5. Stir in the lemon juice and fish sauce
6. If you want a slightly thicker sauce, stir in ½ teaspoon of flour mixed with water as you finish simmering the sauce
7. Cool, then bottle and store at room temperature for two or three days

Sweet Chilli Sauce
This is made from sweeter chillies and isn't designed as a hot sauce. It is popular in Asian cooking or as a dipping sauce. For a slightly hotter sauce, leave the chilli seeds in. Remove them if you want a milder sauce.

Ingredients:
- 2 hot red chillies (e.g., Thai, cayenne, jalapeño, etc.)
- 3 garlic cloves (peeled)
- 180ml/¾ cup water
- 120ml/½ cup sugar
- 60ml/¼ cup vinegar
- 2 tablespoons water
- 1 tablespoon cornstarch
- ½ teaspoon salt

Method:
1. Put the sugar, 180ml/¾ cup of water, vinegar, garlic, salt, and chillies into a food processor and blend into a puree
2. Transfer to a large pan and bring to the boil
3. Simmer for 3-5 minutes until the sauce starts to thicken, and the chillies soften
4. Mix the cornstarch with the two tablespoons of water to make a paste
5. Whisk this into the sauce
6. Boil for about a minute, stirring occasionally
7. Remove from the heat, cool, bottle and store in your refrigerator

How to Dry Chillis

One of the most popular ways of storing chillies is to dry them. These can be used whole or ground into a powder for storage and cooking. It gives you more flexibility in how you use the chillies later in the year and the drying chillies themselves look really good.

Basic Drying Method
This is the basic method for air drying chillies. It works very well, though keep checking your chillies and any that show any sign of rot need to be removed and either discarded or used immediately. This method makes for a nice colourful display, but it will take up space in your home.

1. Remove any dirt from the chilli peppers
2. Wash each pepper thoroughly, putting any damaged peppers to one side for immediate use

3. Dry the peppers
4. Place on a wire rack in a well ventilated, dry room and leave for several weeks until dry
5. Alternatively, string them up with an inch gap between each chilli, and hang them to dry somewhere warm and well ventilated

Once they are dry, you can leave them hanging as ornaments, store them or ground them into chilli powder.

Oven Drying Chillies

A quicker method is to dry your chillies in an oven, This method works well, but it does take several hours during which you cannot use your oven for anything else which may be an inconvenience.

1. Wash your chillies, removing any damaged ones for immediate use
2. Cut each chilli in half lengthwise
3. Arrange the chillies on a baking sheet
4. Put in an oven at 38-57°C/100-135°F, leaving the door cracked open to allow air to circulate
5. Leave in the oven for several hours until dry

Drying Chillies in a Dehydrator

This requires you to own a dehydrator, but is the easiest and most reliable method of drying chillies. This involves a separate kitchen gadget that will dehydrate your chillies slowly over the course of 12-24 hours.

As before, wash the chillies first, removing any damaged ones and then pat them dry with paper towels. Slice them up for faster dehydration, cut them in half or leave them whole, though that will take longer for them to dry the larger they are.

Remove from the dehydrator when completely dry and process or store. Try to make sure the chillies are all about the same size. If you have some big chillies and some small ones then they will be ready at different times. When drying chillies of different sizes, remove the smaller ones first and leave the larger ones in for longer.

Making a Chilli Ristra

A ristra is a traditional way to dry chillies for use later in the year. They are believed to have originated in South America, the home of the chilli. In some areas they are considered to bring good luck to the home yet in many others they are used purely as a decoration.

There are lots of different ways to make a ristra, all slightly different from each other. They work best with varieties that produce long, thin fruit such as cayenne chillies. Varieties with more flesh, such as the jalapeño have more of a chance of rotting rather than drying because of their thickness. If you are going to dry larger chillies, then put them somewhere with plenty of sun and good air circulation which will give them more of a chance to dry completely.

Although there are many different methods of making a ristra, this is the quickest and easiest. It's the best way for you to start and as you get used to making them, you can try some of the other, more traditional methods.

To make your ristra you will need the following equipment:

1. Some fishing line
2. A large sewing needle
3. Plenty of fresh chillies

The chillies need to have some green stem above the fruit, which is where you thread them. When you harvest the chillies, leave about ½" or so of stem on each one.

Put a large knot in one end of the fishing line, tying it multiple times if necessary to get a large enough knot. Thread the needle on to the other end.

Then thread the chillies on to the fishing line through the stem. The angle you thread the chilli stem will determine the shape of the ristra. For a good shape, hold the needle upright, pointing to the sky and thread the chilli at a 45° angle with the stem being higher up than the pod. Push the chillies down and around, so there are no gaps.

Once it is finished, hang it somewhere that gets a lot of light and heat. For most of us, this is in a south-facing window, but for those of you lucky enough to live in a hotter country, you can hang it on a sunny porch.

During the drying process, the chillies darken. Check the ristra regularly and remove any pods that look like they are developing mould. If your pods are growing mould, then move the ristra to somewhere with better ventilation until the chillies are completely dried.

SMOKING CHILLIES

Another great way to preserve your chillies is by smoking them. This can enhance their flavour and allows them to be stored for longer. The chipotle pepper, which is very popular in American cuisine, is a smoked jalapeño pepper. It is a good way to store your peppers and one that many people do not consider doing at home.

Smoked peppers can be used instead of fresh or even roasted in any dish to give it a smoky flavour. Once smoked, a chilli can be ground into a powder which can be used instead of normal chilli powder. It is great for seasonings, rubs and wonderful on grilled meats, where its unusual flavour will attract attention.

The process of smoking chillies is very easy indeed, though you will need a smoker.

1. Wash and thoroughly dry your peppers, discarding any that are damaged or have any signs of rot (these can be used immediately rather than be thrown away).
2. Slice the peppers in half and, if desired, remove the innards, which is where most of the heat is. Thicker walled peppers can be cut into smaller pieces or even rings to allow the smoke to get into more of the pepper.
3. Heat your smoker to 93°C/200°F.
4. Put the peppers on a tray or aluminium foil, so you don't lose them through the grates and put them in the smoker.
5. Follow the smoker instructions to maintain a constant temperature
6. Use your preferred wood for your smoker, such as hickory, mesquite or maple wood.

7. Smoke your chillies for three hours, allowing the smoke to penetrate the peppers. After this time, the chillies will be smoked, but thicker walled peppers will not be completely dried out. Thinner walled chillies can be smoked for less time if you do not want them completely dry.

Once the smoking process is complete, you can preserve your chillies in oil, freeze them or keep them in your refrigerator where they will need using within a few days.

Alternatively, finish drying your smoked chillies in a dehydrator, which will dry them completely. They will need 8 to 10 hours, depending on the size of the peppers and the wall thickness, to dry completely. Set them at a temperature of around 52°C/125°F for best results. Once completely dried, store the chillies in sealed containers until used.

If you have dried the chillies completely then you can use them as is or you can rehydrate them in hot water before using them if you prefer softer chillies. Remember, even when smoked, hot chillies will still be hot. Use gloves to handle super-hot chillies to protect your skin and sensitive areas.

PICKLING CHILLIES

A popular method of preserving chillies is to pickle them. Pickling works with all types of chilli, whether they have thick or thin walls and is a traditional method of storing food, using the acid of the pickling liquid to kill bacteria and preserve the chillies.

Pickled chillies can look very attractive on your shelf, particularly when a variety of coloured chillies are pickled in an ornate jar. This method preserves the chilli in its original form and uses salt and vinegar to preserve the pods for anything up to a year and sometimes more.

As with any other method of preserving, make sure you clean and wash your chillies thoroughly before use. Any fruits that are damaged or have any rot should not be pickled, being put to one side for use over the next few days.

Chillies can be pickled whole, halved, quartered or sliced. Whichever method you use, if you are cutting the chillies, ensure you use a sharp, sterilised knife to reduce the chances of introducing bacteria into the chillies.

Pickling Vinegar
Any vinegar can be used to pickled your chillies so long as it has at least 5% acid. A normal malt (brown) vinegar can be used, or pickling vinegar can be purchased which contain a mixture of herbs and spices. Many people use brown vinegar and add their own spices, if they add any, for additional flavour.

Table and Pickling Salt
You may be forgiven for thinking that salt is salt, but there is a difference between table salt and pickling salt. Pickling salt has finer grains than table salt and is not iodised during manufacture. Because table salt is usually iodised, it can affect the taste of your chillies, leaving a bitter aftertaste. Pickling salt does not clump up during the preserving process.

Storage Jars
Glass jars with lids are best for storing your pickled chillies. Remember to clean and sterilise the lids, jars and seals before use. Kilner type jars are ideal, though any jar will do. Many people will keep jars from store bought products and reuse them. I often buy pickled beetroot, onions or gherkins and keep the empty jars for use in preserving my own produce. Friends and family will keep their jars for me, though if I am selling or gifting pickled chillies I buy ornate jars, so they look good. Sterilise the jars either by putting them through a hot dishwasher cycle, washing in boiling water or cooking in the oven.

Soft or Crisp Pickles
Pickled chillies can be soft or crisp, depending on how you prepare them. For softer chillies, put them in the boiling pickling mixture halfway through the boiling process. The later in the boiling process you put the chillies in, the crisper they will become. For very crisp chillies, put them in the pan once the mixture has boiled.

Basic Pickling Method
This is a basic method of pickling chillies.

1. Wash the chillies in salt water and put to one side
2. Heat 1 litre/2.2 pints of white wine vinegar with five tablespoons of apple cider vinegar
3. To sweeten the mixture, if you prefer, add up to three teaspoons of granulated (white) sugar and stir until it dissolves
4. Bring the mixture to the boil
5. While waiting, use a sterilised needle to poke a small hole in the tip of each chilli
6. Add 4 or 5 bay leaves to the liquid and turn the heat off

7. Add the chillies, stir well and leave for ten minutes
8. Pour into jars and leave to cool fully
9. Once cooled, seal the lids and refrigerate
10. Leave for two weeks for the flavour to mature before using

For softer chillies, add them to the boiling liquid and boil for a few minutes.

Crisp Chilli Pickling Method
This is a great way to make very crisp chillies.

1. Soak the chillies in a mixture of water and pickling salt for 24 hours
2. Rinse the chillies
3. Using a sterilised needle, poke a small hole in the tip of each chilli
4. Put 700ml/3 cups of vinegar, 700ml/3 cups of water, and 3 teaspoons of pickling salt into a pan and bring to the boil
5. Almost fill a jar with the chillies, leaving 4cm/1½" space from the lid
6. Pour the boiling pickling mixture into the jar and leave to cool
7. Tap the jar gently on the counter to remove any air bubbles
8. When cooled, seal the jar and store in the refrigerator
9. Leave for a minimum of two weeks before use to allow the flavour to mature

These can be preserved for longer by using canning methods to boil and seal the jars. In this case, the pickled chillies will last for months and often over a year.

Making a Chilli Oil

Chilli oils are popular in cooking and a great way to store your chillies. Chinese cookery makes particular use of chilli oil, but it can be added to pretty much anything that you cook with oil.

A chilli oil is, in its simplest form, a vegetable oil that has been infused with chilli peppers. You can make it has hot or as mild as you want using any combination of peppers to give it the flavour that you want. Ideally, you want a neutral tasting oil so that the taste of the chillies comes through. Canola oil is one of the most popular base oils, though peanut oil is also popular. Olive oil can be used too, as can sesame oil.

The general process for making a chilli oil is quite easy; heat the oil, add seasoning and chillies and leave to cool. But let's go into more detailed instructions for making your own chilli oil.

Ingredients:
- 240ml/1 cup canola oil (substitute if required for any neutral oil such as olive oil, peanut oil, etc.)
- 3 tablespoons dried chilli peppers (crushed)
- Pinch of salt

Method:
1. Add all of the ingredients to a saucepan and stir well
2. Heat on a medium to low heat, stirring often, for 5 minutes (simmer for longer for a stronger flavour)
3. Make sure that the oil does not smoke. If it does start to smoke, remove the pan from the heat to allow the temperature to reduce. The idea is to simmer the oil to infuse the flavours of the chillies
4. Remove from the heat and leave to cool to room temperature
5. When cooled, bottle and seal
6. Refrigerate and use within a month

This oil can be flavoured with other ingredients too such as garlic, shallots, ginger, soy sauce, bay leaves, peppercorns, star anise and more. It's a good opportunity to make your own, unique chilli oil.

Freezing Chillies

One of the easiest ways to preserve chillies is to freeze them. The downside of this is that you are limited in what you can use the chillies for once you remove them from the freezer. Frozen chillies usually end up a little bit soft and squishy, having lost the crunch many people like. As they have a high water content, they unfortunately, do not freeze particularly well. They are usually added, while still frozen, to dishes and cooked rather than used raw or in any other way.

Chillies are best frozen as soon as you can after harvesting. Typically, you will slice them before freezing into the size you usually see sliced chillies in the stores. Leaving them whole encourages uneven freezing and can damage the chilli as some parts freeze before others. Cut out any damaged or soft parts of the chilli, remove the seeds and cut off the top with the stalk.

There are two schools of thoughts regarding freezing chillies and proponents of each method will argue until they are blue in the face about which method is best. You can blanch the chillies prior to freezing or just cut, wash and dry, and then freeze.

The advantage of blanching is that it kills any harmful bacteria before you put the chillies into the freezer, which has its obvious benefits. The downside is it can make the chilli that little bit softer after defrosting. To blanch your chillies, just put them in boiling water for 60 to 90 seconds and then cool immediately by plunging them into iced water or holding them under cold running water.

Whether you blanch them or not, they are then spread out on baking trays, making sure they do not touch and the trays are put in the freezer. When the chillies are completely frozen, remove them from the trays and put them in freezer bags. Label the bags, then return them to the freezer for long term storage. Make sure you write the date of freezing and the variety on the bag to avoid confusion later on.

It is very simple but only do this is for chillies that you are going to use directly in meals. Preserving chillies using some of the other methods gives you a lot more flexibility in how you use the chillies later on. Because the freezing process damages the cells of the chilli peppers, you are very limited in how they can be used once they are defrosted.

How to Make Chilli Powder

Chilli powder is used in many different dishes, and it is one of the easiest ways of preserving your chillies for use later in the year. It is very easy to make and stores well. You can mix a variety of different types of chillies for a more complex flavour, or you can use a single type if you prefer. This can be made as hot or as mild as you want, depending on the type of chilli used.

To start with, wash the chillies well and dry them. Remove the stems and cut them in half lengthways. The seeds can be left in place for a hotter powder, but can give it a slightly bitter taste, or they can be removed for a slightly milder powder. Personally, I prefer to remove the seeds and use hotter chillies if I want extra heat, though that is up to you.

Next, the chillies need to be dried. This is easiest in a food dehydrator, but they can be dried in an oven if you don't own a dehydrator. Lay the chillies flat on a baking tray and put in an oven heated to 150°C/300°F. Check the chillies after a few minutes, removing any that are dry. Larger chillies or those with thicker walls take longer to dry. Keep checking the chillies every few minutes and remove those that are completely dry and put them to one side to cool.

To round out the flavour, add a few cumin seeds to the chilli powder at a ratio of one part cumin to ten parts chilli. Toast the cumin seeds in a hot, dry skillet for a couple of minutes. When they start to darken, remove them from the heat and grind to a powder using a mortar and pestle.

Finally, the chillies and the cumin powder are ground together using a blender (pulse for 30 seconds at a time), chilli grinder or a coffee grinder.

The great thing about making your own chilli powder is that you can change the flavour of the powder by using different types of chillies. Using smoked jalapeños gives the powder a smoky flavour. Add some habaneros gives the powder a very fruity flavour. If you grow different types of chilli, then you can play around with different combinations to make a unique chilli powder that suits your needs and tastes.

Home-made chilli powder stores for about a year in an airtight jar and kept somewhere cool and dry. Chilli powder can also be frozen in an airtight bag, though using a vacuum sealer is much better and can double the storage time.

Making your own chilli powder is surprisingly easy to do. It's a great way of storing your home-grown chillies and wonderful to add to the meals you are cooking.

RECIPES FOR CHILLIES

One of the most popular uses for chillies isn't for making sauce, that tends to be more for the chilli-head, but for adding to meals. There are a huge number of uses for chillies, as they are such a versatile vegetable. There are so many different varieties of chilli that can completely change the taste of a dish by using different types of chilli or even a combination of different chillies. A Habanero chilli, for example, gives a dish a fruity flavour combined with the heat of a chilli whereas a jalapeño only provides heat without the fruity taste.

All of these recipes will recommend a type of chilli to use, but feel free to adjust the variety based on the heat level you want for the dish. Feel free to use hotter chillies if you prefer hotter dishes or use cooler chillies for dishes that won't blow your head off.

Tailgate Chilli
This is a great chilli recipe that you can make at home, or when you go out to an event and reheat it. It's a traditional American dish that would be made on a cooker on the tailgate of a truck in the car park of a sports arena. It is simple to make, feeds plenty of people, and you can use whatever chilli peppers you have to hand. Add some habaneros for a fruity heat or some jalapeños for less heat. This dish will take about two and a half hours to make.

Ingredients:
- 900g/2lb ground beef chuck
- 450g/1lb Italian sausage
- 8oz cheddar cheese (shredded)
- 2 x 800g/28oz can diced tomatoes (with juice)
- 3 x 425g/15oz can chilli beans (drained)

- 425g/15oz can chilli beans in a spicy sauce
- 170g/6oz tomato paste
- 1 large onion (chopped)
- 3 celery stalks (chopped)
- Green bell pepper (de-seeded and chopped)
- Red bell pepper (de-seeded and chopped)
- 2 x green chilli peppers (de-seeded and chopped)
- 1 tablespoon bacon bits
- 1 tablespoon Worcestershire sauce
- 1 tablespoon fresh garlic (minced)
- 1 tablespoon dried oregano
- 4 beef bouillon cubes
- 120ml/½ cup beer
- 60ml/¼ cup chilli powder (can be home-made for extra heat)
- 2 teaspoons ground cumin
- 1 teaspoon ground black pepper
- 1 teaspoon salt
- 1 teaspoon paprika
- 1 teaspoon white (granulated) sugar
- 1 teaspoon cayenne pepper
- 300g/10½oz corn chips

Method:
1. Heat a large pot over a medium to high heat and add the ground beef chuck and sausage
2. Cook, stirring often until brown all over
3. Drain excess fat
4. Add both types of chilli beans, the diced tomatoes, and the tomato paste
5. Stir well and cook for a 1-2 minutes
6. Add the celery, bell peppers, chilli peppers, onion, bacon bits, beer, and bouillon, stirring well
7. Add the rest of the ingredients to season and stir
8. Cover and simmer, occasionally stirring, for two to three hours until evenly cooked and the flavours have combined, the slow simmering gives the chilli its taste
9. Season further with salt, pepper or chilli powder as required a few minutes before serving
10. Serve in bowls topped with shredded Cheddar cheese and corn chips

Spicy Sweet Potato Chips

This simple dish can be made in about half an hour and is great as a side dish. Make this on your barbecue or indoors in your oven. Bake at 220°C/400°F on a greased tray for 20-30 minutes.

Ingredients:
- 2 sweet potatoes (peeled and sliced into ¼" slices)
- 60ml/¼ cup extra virgin olive oil
- 2 tablespoons garlic (minced)
- Juice of 1 lime
- 1½ teaspoons ground cumin
- 1 teaspoon home-made chilli powder (as hot or mild as you desire)
- Salt and pepper to taste

Method:
1. Preheat your barbecue on to a medium/high heat and oil the cooking grate
2. In a large bowl, mix everything except the sweet potatoes, ensuring the ingredients are thoroughly combined
3. Add the sweet potatoes to the bowl and stir, ensuring they are completely coated with the marinade
4. Cook on your grill for 15 to 20 minutes, turning every 5 minutes, until tender in the middle and crisp on the outside

Home-Made Fajita Seasoning

Everyone loves fajitas, so instead of buying your seasoning from the store, make your own at home. It's simple to do, and you can use your home-made chilli powder to give it a proper kick. This is a great recipe that can be made in just a few minutes

Ingredients:
- 1 tablespoon cornstarch
- 2 teaspoons home-made chilli powder
- 1 teaspoon paprika
- 1 teaspoon salt
- 1 teaspoon granulated (white) sugar
- ½ teaspoon garlic powder
- ½ teaspoon onion powder
- ¼ teaspoon cayenne pepper
- ½ teaspoon ground cumin

Method:
1. Add all the ingredients to a small bowl
2. Mix well until thoroughly combined

Chilli Jam

This preserve is one of the best ways of storing your chillies and will keep for six to twelve months. It can be used in pretty much any dish to give it a bit of extra spice. The secret to success with this dish is not to overcook it. Be aware that it is not going to set like jam does as there is no pectin in chillies. Taste the jam as you are cooking it and use your best judgment to know when it is ready.

Ingredients:
- 1¼kg/2¾lb fresh tomatoes
- 825g/1¾lb granulated (white) sugar
- 125g/4½oz fresh ginger (peeled and grated)
- 125g/4½oz garlic (crushed)
- 60g/2¼oz red chillies (stems removed)
- 30ml/1fl oz red wine vinegar
- 2 tablespoons Worcestershire sauce
- ½ tablespoon salt

Method:
1. Put the chillies and the tomatoes into your food processor (in batches if necessary)
2. Process until smooth, then pour into a large saucepan
3. Add the remaining ingredients and bring slowly to the boil, stirring often until the sugar dissolves fully
4. Cook at a fast simmer for about an hour, stirring more often as time progresses
5. Once the jam has thickened and has a good colour, remove it from the heat, pour into sterilised jars and store in a cool, dark place

Chill Jam version 2

This is another recipe for chilli jam, but one which produces a solid jam, or jelly, rather than a runny one as per the previous recipe. This looks great as the bits of chilli end up suspended in the jam and it tastes divine. Leave this to stand for a month before using to allow the flavours to mature. Use within a year and once opened, refrigerate and use within a month. Feel free to use whatever chillies you want in this or to replace the bell peppers with other chilli peppers to give the dish a bit of a kick. Combining a fruity chilli such as the Habanero with a hot chilli such as a jalapeño can make for a really interesting taste.

Ingredients:
- 150g/5¼oz red chilli peppers (deseeded and quartered)
- 150g/5¼oz red bell peppers (deseeded and cut into chunks)
- 1kg/2.2lbs jam sugar (or regular granulated sugar plus liquid/powdered pectin to make the jam set)
- 600ml/2½ cups apple cider vinegar

Method:
1. Sterilise your jars and leave them to cool
2. Process the chillies and bell pepper in your food processor until they are finely chopped, not pureed
3. Heat the sugar and vinegar in a medium sized pan on a low heat, until it has dissolved – don't stir it at this point
4. Add the peppers to the saucepan
5. Bring to the boil and leave at a rolling boil for 10 minutes
6. Remove the pan from the heat and leave to cool, so the liquid thickens
7. After around 40 minutes, the pepper pieces will be evenly dispersed in the jelly
8. You can stir at this point if you want to spread out the chilli pieces
9. Pour into your jars carefully, then seal them

Huevos Rancheros

This is a popular dish that is delicious. The combination of eggs and chilli set each other off well. Use whatever chillies you want to make it as hot as you like. To give the dish even more heat, leave the seeds in the chillies. If you want to make this even better, add some chorizo to give it more flavour as this goes well with the chillies. This recipe makes two servings.

Ingredients
- 400g/14oz can chopped/diced tomatoes
- 4 eggs
- 2 tortillas
- 1 garlic clove (finely chopped)
- 1 hot chilli such as Scotch bonnet (deseeded and chopped)
- ½ onion (chopped)
- 2 tablespoons sour cream
- 1 tablespoon extra-virgin olive oil
- 1 teaspoon tomato puree
- ½ teaspoon ground cumin

Method:
1. Heat the oil in a large saucepan
2. Cook the onion until softened on a low heat for 5 minutes
3. Add the chilli and garlic and cook for a further 2 to 4 minutes until soft but not coloured
4. Increase the heat and add the ground cumin and tomato puree
5. Allow to bubble for a minute then add the tomatoes
6. Cook, stirring often, on a medium heat for 20 minutes, adding some water if it starts to dry out
7. Once the sauce has reduced, make four wells in it and break the eggs into these holes
8. Fry the eggs, occasionally basting the yolk with the tomato sauce
9. Warm the tortillas in another pan and place on warmed plates
10. When the eggs are cooked to your preference, spoon two on to each tortilla, sharing the sauce between them and putting a teaspoon of sour cream onto each egg

Chilli Cheese Toasties

A toasted cheese sandwich is great at pretty much any time, and the chillies add a welcome kick to this snack. Use whatever chillies you want to make this to your taste. You can use any cheese you like in your toastie, though I can recommend cheddar, which melts in a very satisfying way or paneer, which doesn't melt the same but has an interesting taste and texture. This makes enough for four people.

Ingredients:
- 8 slices of bread (buttered on both sides)
- 1 tomato (diced)
- 2 or 3 chillies of your choice (finely chopped)

- ½ red onion (finely chopped)
- 175g/6¼oz cheese (grated or crumbled)
- A handful of chopped coriander (cilantro) leaves
- 1 teaspoon chaat masala
- Salt and black pepper to taste

Chutney Ingredients:
- 1 chilli (roughly chopped)
- 3 tablespoons lemon juice
- 1 teaspoon ground cumin (dry roasted)
- 2 large handfuls of coriander (cilantro) leaves

Method:
1. Make the chutney by putting all the ingredients in your food processor and blending until finely chopped. Add a little water and blend further until smooth
2. Spread the chutney on four slices of bread
3. Mix the cheese, coriander, tomato, onion, and chillies in a small bowl
4. Divide this evenly between the slices of bread that have chutney on
5. Season to taste with salt, pepper and chaat masala
6. Put a slice of buttered bread on each of the slices of bread that has the cheese and chutney on
7. Grill on a medium temperature until the cheese melts and the bread turns a golden brown colour
8. Serve immediately with your favourite ketchup

Chilli and Apple Stew

This is a lovely aromatic stew that combines spice and sweet very well. Use your choice of chillies in this dish, though milder chillies work well. Look for a chilli with a fruity flavour as well as some spice to really bring out the flavours in this recipe, which makes enough for two people. Serve with some home-made crusty bread.

Ingredients:
- 10 new potatoes
- 3 garlic cloves (finely chopped)
- 2 shallots (peeled and chopped)
- 2 large red chillies (finely sliced)
- 1 head of celery (top and tailed, then roughly chopped)
- 1 cinnamon stick
- 1 apple (peeled, cored and diced)

- 400g/14oz tin diced tomatoes
- 2 tablespoons extra-virgin olive oil
- 1 tablespoon fresh tarragon (chopped)
- 1 teaspoon black treacle or brown sugar
- Large knob of butter
- Pinch of red chilli flakes
- Salt and black pepper to taste

Method:
1. Heat the oil in a pan and fry the shallots until they start to caramelise
2. Add the chilli, garlic and the cinnamon stick, frying for another couple of minutes, stirring regularly
3. Add the apple and celery, cooking on a medium heat, stirring occasionally, for five to seven minutes until softened
4. Add the treacle and tomatoes, then season well
5. Cook for a further 30 minutes, stirring occasionally
6. Towards the end of this 30 minutes, stir the tarragon in
7. Meanwhile, boil the potatoes
8. Position the potatoes in the middle of each plate and surround them with the stew. Place a knob of butter on the potatoes and sprinkle the whole dish with chilli flakes

Stuffed Jalapeño Peppers

These are a favourite with many people and are very easy to make as a snack or starter. Of course, you can add a twist to this by using chillies other than jalapeño's, and even adding some chilli to the cream cheese stuffing for an extra kick.

Ingredients:
- 20 jalapeño chillies
- 100g/3½oz plain (all-purpose) flour
- 75g/2½oz panko breadcrumbs
- 2 eggs (lightly beaten)
- 1 teaspoon smoked paprika

- Vegetable oil for frying (about 1 litre/2.2 pints will be enough)

Stuffing Ingredients:
- 150g/5¼oz full fat cream cheese
- 50g/1¾oz sultanas (roughly chopped)
- 50g/1¾oz parmesan cheese (grated)
- Salt and pepper to taste

Method:
1. Make the stuffing by mixing all the stuffing ingredients together in a small bowl, then putting it to one side
2. Bring a large pan of water to the boil
3. Add the jalapeño chillies and cook them for 60 seconds, then remove them, drain and leave to cool until they can be comfortably handled
4. Use a sharp knife to cut the chilli on one side lengthwise, from top to bottom – avoid cutting all the way down, aim for a cut of about three quarters the length of the chilli
5. Use a spoon or butter knife to flick out the membrane and seeds carefully
6. Put a teaspoon or two of the cream cheese mix in each chilli and squeeze the cut together, so it seals and looks uncut
7. Mix the flour and paprika together
8. Put the egg, breadcrumbs, and flour on to three separate plates or shallow bowls
9. Dip each chilli into the flour first, then the egg and finally the breadcrumbs, setting each coated chilli to one side
10. Heat the oil in a saucepan ready to deep fry the chillies
11. Use a slotted spoon to lower three or four chillies at a time into the oil
12. Cook until golden brown, around 2 minutes
13. Remove with a slotted spoon, drain on kitchen paper and keep warm (in the oven) while the rest of the chillies are cooked

Scorching Pork Sliders
This is not a recipe for the faint hearted. The ghost peppers give these pork sliders a real kick, though feel free to use a milder pepper to save yourself from their heat. A habanera or even sweet bell peppers will work in this dish, allowing you to tailor it to your personal preferences. These are topped with spicy mayo and quick pickled peppers, both of which are very easy to make.

Slider Ingredients:
- 340g/12oz ground pork or plant based alternative
- 6 slider buns
- 3 tablespoons Harissa or guajillo paste
- 2 tablespoons breadcrumbs
- 1 ghost chilli (minced)
- 1 teaspoon garlic powder
- 1 teaspoon extra-virgin olive oil
- ½ teaspoon ground cumin
- Salt and pepper to taste

Mayo Ingredients
- 120ml/½ cup mayo
- 1 teaspoon white wine vinegar
- 1 teaspoon Harissa/guajillo paste

Quick Pickled Pepper Ingredients
- 240ml/1 cup white vinegar
- 1 tablespoon granulated (white) sugar
- Sliced chilli peppers (any, depending on the heat level you like or sweet bell peppers)

Method:
1. Make the mayo by whisking together all the mayo ingredients in a small bowl
2. Make the quick pickled peppers by boiling the chillies and sugar in a pan, covering with vinegar, then simmering for 5 minutes before removing from the heat
3. Add the ground pork, guajillo paste, ghost chilli, seasonings, and breadcrumbs to a bowl and mix, taking care not to over mix otherwise the burgers become a little mealy
4. Form the meat into six patties; each one should be about 60g/2oz
5. Put on a plate, cover and refrigerate for 30 minutes
6. Heat your grill pan to a medium heat and coat with olive oil
7. Cook for 3 to 4 minutes per side, until cooked through
8. Add the patties to the buns, topping with the mayo and pickled peppers

Cajun Stuffed Poblano Peppers

These are very tasty and must for everyone to try. The peppers are stuffed with Cajun seasoned shrimp and absolutely delicious. This recipe takes about 55 minutes to prepare and cook, making enough for two servings. The Manchego cheese can be substituted for something similar such as gouda, gruyere, emmental, edam or cheddar.

Ingredients:
- 227g/8oz shrimp (deveined and peeled)
- 114g/4oz goats cheese
- 114g/4oz Manchego cheese (shredded)
- 1 large onion (chopped)
- 10 large basil leaves (shredded)
- 2 large poblano peppers
- 2 garlic cloves (chopped)
- 1 jalapeño chilli (chopped)
- 1 tablespoon hot sauce
- 1 tablespoon Cajun seasoning
- 2 teaspoons extra-virgin olive oil
- Fresh coriander (cilantro) (chopped – for topping)

Method:
1. Roast the poblano chillies in your oven on the grill/broil setting for 15 minutes, until the skins char and puff up, though make sure they are not too close to the heat source so they do not burn. Halfway through cooking, flip them to ensure both sides are cooked
2. Remove from the heat, cool until you can handle them, then remove the skins
3. Slice the poblanos in half lengthwise
4. Remove the insides, being careful not to damage the skin, then put on a large baking dish
5. Put the shrimp into a large mixing bowl with a tablespoon of olive oil and toss with the Cajun seasoning until thoroughly coated
6. Heat a teaspoon of oil in a pan on a medium heat
7. Cook the onion and jalapeño chillies for 5 minutes, until soft
8. Add the garlic and cook for 1 minute
9. Put this mixture into a large mixing bowl
10. Put the shrimp into the pan and cook for 2 minutes per side, until cooked through
11. Cool, then chop the shrimp and add to your mixing bowl
12. Add the basil, cheeses and the hot sauce, then mix well

13. Scoop the mixture into the peppers, pushing down lightly
14. Bake at 190°C/375°F for 20 to 30 minutes
15. Serve topped with coriander, hot sauce, and chilli flakes

Scorching Mango Salsa

This is a great take on the traditional salsa, with the sweetness of the mango, offsetting the heat of the chillies. Although this recipe uses very hot chilli peppers, feel free to adjust the combination of chillies to your own tastes. This salsa takes around 35 minutes to prepare and cook.

Ingredients:
- 4 garlic cloves (chopped)
- 2 small mangos (peeled, destoned and chopped)
- 2 serrano chillies (chopped)
- 2 medium red tomatoes (chopped)
- 1 small sweet onion (chopped)
- 1 habanero chilli (chopped)
- 1 jalapeño chilli (chopped)
- 120ml/½ cup red wine vinegar
- 4g/¼ cup fresh chopped coriander (cilantro)
- Juice of 1 lime
- Salt and pepper to taste

Method:
1. Put all the ingredients into your food processor
2. Pulse several times until you achieve your preferred consistency
3. Pour this into a pan and bring to a quick boil
4. Reduce the heat and simmer for 20 minutes
5. Cool and then store in your refrigerator in an airtight container
6. Leave for a day for the flavours to mature

Spicy Meatballs

This is a great meatball recipe with a tasty chipotle and lime sauce. It takes about 1 hour, 20 minutes to make and serves eight people.

Meatball Ingredients:
- 454g/1lb ground beef
- 454g/1lb ground pork
- 6 garlic cloves (chopped)
- 2 jalapeño chillies (chopped)
- 2 eggs

- 1 large onion (chopped)
- 120ml/½ cup chicken broth
- 50g/½ cup panko breadcrumbs
- 2 tablespoons chipotle sauce
- 1 tablespoon taco seasoning
- 1 teaspoon ground cumin

Sauce Ingredients:
- 140g/5oz can chipotle sauce
- 2 garlic cloves (chopped)
- 1 small onion (chopped)
- 1 jalapeño (chopped)
- 120ml/½ cup chicken broth
- 2 tablespoons honey
- 2 tablespoons tomato paste
- 1 tablespoon extra-virgin olive oil
- Juice of 1 lime

Method:
1. Preheat your oven to 200°C/400°F
2. In a large bowl, mix the pork, beef, eggs, peppers, garlic, onion, broth, seasonings and chipotle sauce. Hand mix, rather than use a mixer and ensure it is well combined, but not overmixed
3. Form the mixture into meatballs about 4cm/1½" in diameter. It should make around 40 meatballs
4. Put on a lightly oiled baking sheet and cook for 30-40 minutes, until cooked through
5. Meanwhile, heat a large pot with the olive oil on a medium heat to make the sauce, timing it to be ready when the meatballs are cooked
6. Cook the onions and jalapeños for 5 minutes, until soft
7. Add the garlic and cook for a further minute

8. Add the rest of the ingredients except the lime juice and simmer for 10 minutes
9. Add the lime juice, stir briefly then add the meatballs
10. Simmer for 5 minutes, regularly spooning the sauce over the meatballs

Southwest Style Cheesy Dip

This is a great dip to serve with nachos and with the mango salsa mentioned previously. It is very easy to make, taking about 20 minutes and is perfect for entertaining.

Ingredients:

- 454g/16oz sour cream
- 425g/15oz can black beans (drained)
- 226g/8oz cream cheese
- 118g/1 cup cheddar cheese (shredded)
- 118g/1 cup pepper jack cheese (shredded)
- 90g/1 cup parmesan cheese (shredded)
- 1 to 2 jalapeño chillies (diced)
- 4 tablespoons unsalted butter
- 1 tablespoon garlic powder
- 1 tablespoon chilli powder (mild or hot depending on personal preference)
- 1 teaspoon ground cumin
- Salt and pepper to taste

Method:
1. Put the butter, sour cream and cream cheese into a saucepan and heat slowly, stirring regularly until it becomes very creamy
2. Add the jalapeño peppers and stir well
3. Swirl in the cheese, a little at the time, constantly stirring until the cheeses have completely melted
4. Add the rest of the ingredients and season to taste
5. Simmer for 5 minutes, stirring regularly, then serve

Endnote

Chillies are a great vegetable to grow. They are very popular, used in a wide range of cuisines and have a fanatical following across the world. Growers vie with each other to create the hottest chilli or chilli sauce, and there is a lot of prestige associated with growing new, hot varieties.

Growing chillies at home doesn't have to be competitive; you can grow them purely because you like chillies and want to experience more flavour, heat, and variety than you can find in the stores. Typically, a supermarket will stock one or maybe two varieties, one of which will be plain, mild chillies and the other a hotter variety such as Scotch bonnet or jalapeño. If you can find an Asian or Mexican vegetable stand, then you may be fortunate enough to discover other chilli varieties too, including some unusual ones used in their cooking.

The beauty of growing chillies at home is that you can grow varieties that you cannot find in the shop and those that you enjoy or have always wanted to try. You can grow a couple of plants on your kitchen windowsill or dozens of plants in a greenhouse, depending on how many chillies you want. For me, part of the fun is growing hot chillies and allowing my family and friends to try them.

Growing chillies is not that difficult, though the hotter varieties admittedly are more temperamental when it comes to germination and growing environment. The important consideration is that they have quite a long growing season, are very susceptible to cold weather and need warmth to grow. If you live in a temperate climate, then you are unlikely to be able to grow chillies outside. Here, in the northern part of the United Kingdom, I start my chillies off from seed in January indoors, under grow lamps. They are potted on and eventually moved to larger pots and placed in a greenhouse about May. Because the weather is cooler here in the north, they are usually not ready to harvest until August at the very earliest. In hotter climates, chillies will mature much faster and can be grown outside.

Remember that the hotter chilli varieties need more heat to grow successfully. If you are growing something like the Carolina Reaper in a cooler climate, then it will benefit from artificial lighting and heat to mature and produce a good crop of hot chillies.

This book has given you step by step instructions to grow your own chilli plants at home successfully. It is something you can do without the need for expensive, specialist equipment and is a great hobby. Whether you grow lots of your own produce at home or not, chillies are a great addition to your home.

What I like the most about chillies is their sheer versatility. You have the habanero, with a gorgeous combination of fruity flavours with a spicy kick. The jalapeño gives you heat, yet when smoked it becomes the chipotle pepper with a much subtler flavour. In the same family, you have a wide range of sweet bell peppers which are delicious raw or roasted and have barely any heat at all. For the bravest of the brave, you have chillies such as the ghost pepper and the famous Carolina Reaper, designed to make you regret it in the morning.

Growing chillies is fun, and I will tell you now, the first time you see a chilli on one of your plants will be a special moment indeed. Even after all the years I've been growing chillies, this year when I saw the first chilli form on my chocolate habanero plant I got far too excited!

Have great fun growing your chillies, but enjoy using them even more. Whether you choose to pickle them, powder them or cook with them is entirely up to you. All of the recipes in this book can be made with pretty much any chilli you want. Feeling really brave? Try stuffing a habanero instead of a jalapeño, or even a ghost pepper! Enjoy growing and using your chillies with your newfound knowledge and remember, feel free to drop me a line at www.GardeningWithJason.com or through Instagram or Twitter (@allotmentowner). I'd love to see your chilli plants and know what varieties you are growing!

About Jason

Jason has been a keen gardener for over twenty years, having taken on numerous weed infested patches and turned them into productive vegetable gardens.

One of his first gardening experiences was digging over a 400 square foot garden in its entirety and turning it into a vegetable garden, much to the delight of his neighbors who all got free vegetables! It was through this experience that he discovered his love of gardening and started to learn more and more about the subject.

His first encounter with a greenhouse resulted in a tomato infested greenhouse but he soon learnt how to make the most of a greenhouse and now grows a wide variety of plants from grapes to squashes to tomatoes and more. Of course, his wife is delighted with his greenhouse as it means the windowsills in the house are no longer filled with seed trays every spring.

He is passionate about helping people learn to grow their own fresh produce and enjoy the many benefits that come with it, from the exercise of gardening to the nutrition of freshly picked produce. He often says that when you've tasted a freshly picked tomato you'll never want to buy another one from a store again!

Jason is also very active in the personal development community, having written books on self-help, including subjects such as motivation and confidence. He has also recorded over 80 hypnosis programs, being a fully qualified clinical hypnotist which he sells from his website www.MusicForChange.com.

He hopes that this book has been a pleasure for you to read and that you have learned a lot about the subject and welcomes your feedback either directly or through an Amazon review. This feedback is used to improve his books and provide better quality information for his readers.

Jason also loves to grow giant and unusual vegetables and is still planning on breaking the 400lb barrier with a giant pumpkin. He hopes that with his new allotment plot he'll be able to grow even more exciting vegetables to share with his readers.

Other Books By Jason

Please check out my other gardening books on Amazon, available in Kindle and paperback.

A Gardener's Guide to Weeds - How To Use Common Garden Weeds For Food, Health, Beauty And More
Ever wondered about the weeds that take over your garden? You may be surprised to know that these weeds are the ancestors of many of the crops we regularly eat and used to be the staple diet for humans. This book teaches you all about weeds including how to use them in your garden and kitchen and their traditional medicinal uses as well as the folklore and myths associated with them. A fascinating insight into the gardener's foe!

An Allotment Journal – Plan Your Fruit and Vegetable Garden
Learn how to plan your vegetable garden or allotment for success as you discover the techniques for growing a bountiful harvest. Discover how to track what you are growing, where you are growing it and how to make the most of your space. Learn techniques such as crop rotation and succession planting to make the most of your space together with monthly jobs at the allotment, a seed planting schedule plus growing guides for over 50 different vegetables.

An Introduction To Smallholdings – Getting Started On Your Smallholding
Thinking about getting a smallholding? Find out everything you need to consider from the best location to what equipment you need. Talking about everything relating to a smallholding such as how to make an income, what to grow and sell, keeping animals and more, this guide will walk you through everything you must know before living the smallholding dream.

Berry Gardening – The Complete Guide to Berry Gardening from Gooseberries to Boysenberries and More
Who doesn't love fresh berries? Find out how you can grow many of the popular berries at home such as marionberries and blackberries and some of the more unusual like honeyberries and goji berries. A step by step guide to growing your own berries including pruning, propagating and more. Discover how you can grow a wide variety of berries at home in your garden or on your balcony.

Canning and Preserving at Home – A Complete Guide to Canning, Preserving and Storing Your Produce

A complete guide to storing your home-grown fruits and vegetables. Learn everything from how to freeze your produce to canning, making jams, jellies, and chutneys to dehydrating and more. Everything you need to know about storing your fresh produce, including some unusual methods of storage, some of which will encourage children to eat fresh fruit!

Companion Planting Secrets – Organic Gardening to Deter Pests and Increase Yield

Learn the secrets of natural and organic pest control with companion planting. This is a great way to increase your yield, produce better quality plants and work in harmony with nature. By attracting beneficial insects to your garden, you can naturally keep down harmful pests and reduce the damage they cause. You probably grow many of these companion plants already, but by repositioning them, you can benefit from this natural method of gardening.

Container Gardening - Growing Vegetables, Herbs & Flowers in Containers

A step by step guide showing you how to create your very own container garden. Whether you have no garden, little space or you want to grow specific plants, this book guides you through everything you need to know about planting a container garden from the different types of pots, to which plants thrive in containers to handy tips helping you avoid the common mistakes people make with containers..

Cooking With Zucchini - Delicious Recipes, Preserves and More With Courgettes: How To Deal With A Glut Of Zucchini And Love It!

Getting too many zucchinis from your plants? This book teaches you how to grow your own courgettes at home as well as showing you the many different varieties you could grow. Packed full of delicious recipes, you will learn everything from the famous zucchini chocolate cake to delicious main courses, snacks, and Paleo diet friendly raw recipes. The must have guide for anyone dealing with a glut of zucchini.

Environmentally Friendly Gardening - - Your Guide to a Sustainable Eco-Friendly Garden

A guide to making your garden more environmentally friendly, from looking after beneficial insects and wildlife, to saving water and reducing plastic use. There is a lot you can do to reduce your reliance on chemicals and work in harmony with nature, while still having a beautiful and productive garden.

This book details many things you can easily do to become more eco-friendly in your garden.

Greenhouse Gardening - A Beginners Guide to Growing Fruit and Vegetables All Year Round

A complete, step by step guide to owning a greenhouse. Learn everything you need to know from sourcing greenhouses to building foundations to ensuring it survives high winds. This handy guide will teach you everything you need to know to grow a wide range of plants in your greenhouse, including tomatoes, chilies, squashes, zucchini and much more.

Growing Brassicas – Growing Cruciferous Vegetables from Broccoli to Mooli to Wasabi and More

Brassicas are renowned for their health benefits and are packed full of vitamins. They are easy to grow at home, but beset by problems. Find out how you can grow these amazing vegetables at home, including the incredibly beneficial plants broccoli and maca. Includes step by step growing guides plus delicious recipes for every recipe!

Growing Chillies – A Beginners Guide to Growing, Using & Surviving Chillies

Ever wanted to grow super-hot chillies? Or maybe you just want to grow your own chillies to add some flavour to your food? This book is your complete, step-by-step guide to growing chillies at home. With topics from selecting varieties to how to germinate seeds, you will learn everything you need to know to grow chillies successfully, even the notoriously difficult to grow varieties such as Carolina Reaper. With recipes for sauces, meals and making your own chilli powder, you'll find everything you need to know to grow your own chilli plants.

Growing Fruit: The Complete Guide to Growing Fruit at Home

This is a complete guide to growing fruit from apricots to walnuts and everything in between. You will learn how to choose fruit plants, how to grow and care for them, how to store and preserve the fruit and much more. With recipes, advice, and tips this is the perfect book for anyone who wants to learn more about growing fruit at home, whatever their level of experience.

Growing Garlic – A Complete Guide to Growing, Harvesting & Using Garlic

Everything you need to know to grow this popular plant. Whether you are growing normal garlic or elephant garlic for cooking or health, you will find this book contains all the information you need. Traditionally a difficult crop to grow with a long growing season, you'll learn the exact conditions garlic needs, how to avoid the common problems people encounter and how to store your garlic for use all year round. A complete, step-by-step guide showing you precisely how to grow garlic at home.

Growing Giant Pumpkins – How to Grow Massive Pumpkins At Home

A complete step-by-step guide detailing everything you need to know to produce pumpkins weighing hundreds of pounds, if not edging into the thousands! Anyone can grow giant pumpkins at home, and this book gives you the insider secrets of the giant pumpkin growers showing you how to avoid the mistakes people commonly make when trying to grow a giant pumpkin. This is a complete guide detailing everything from preparing the soil to getting the right seeds to germination and caring for your pumpkins.

Growing Herbs – A Beginners Guide To Growing, Using, Harvesting and Storing Herbs

A comprehensive guide to growing herbs at home, detailing 49 different herbs. Learn everything you need to know to grow these herbs from their preferred soil conditions to how to harvest and propagate them and more. Including recipes for health and beauty plus delicious dishes to make in your kitchen. This step-by-step guide is designed to teach you all about growing herbs at home, from a few herbs in containers to a fully-fledged herb garden.

Growing Lavender: Growing, Using, Cooking and Healing with Lavender

A complete guide to growing and using this beautiful plant. Find out about the hundreds of different varieties of lavender and how you can grow this bee friendly plant at home. With hundreds of uses in crafts, cooking and healing, this plant has a long history of association with humans. Discover how you can grow lavender at home and enjoy this amazing herb.

Growing Tomatoes: Your Guide to Growing Delicious Tomatoes

This is the definitive guide to growing delicious and fresh tomatoes at home. Teaching you everything from selecting seeds to planting and caring for your tomatoes as well as diagnosing problems this is the ideal book for anyone who wants to grow their own tomatoes. You will learn the secrets of a successful tomato grower and learn about the many different types of tomato you could grow, most of which are not available in any shops! A comprehensive must have guide.

How to Compost – Turn Your Waste into Brown Gold

This is a complete step by step guide to making your own compost at home. Vital to any gardener, this book will explain everything from setting up your compost heap to how to ensure you get fresh compost in just a few weeks.

You will learn the techniques for producing highly nutritious compost that will help your plants grow while recycling your kitchen waste. A must have handbook for any gardener who wants their plants to benefit from home-made compost.

How to Grow Potatoes - The Guide To Choosing, Planting and Growing in Containers Or the Ground

Learn everything you need to know about growing potatoes at home. Discover the wide variety of potatoes you can grow, many delicious varieties you will never see in the shops. Find out the best way to grow potatoes at home, how to protect your plants from the many pests and diseases and how to store your harvest so you can enjoy fresh potatoes over winter. A complete step by step guide telling you everything you need to know to grow potatoes at home successfully.

Hydroponics: A Beginners Guide to Growing Food without Soil

Hydroponics is growing plants without soil, which is a fantastic idea for indoor gardens. It is surprisingly easy to set up, once you know what you are doing and is significantly more productive and quicker than growing in soil. It doesn't even have to be expensive to get started, and the possibilities are endless. This book will tell you everything you need to know to get started growing flowers, vegetables and fruit hydroponically at home.

Indoor Gardening for Beginners: The Complete Guide to Growing Herbs, Flowers, Vegetables and Fruits in Your House

Discover how you can grow a wide variety of plants in your home. Whether you want to grow herbs for cooking, vegetables or a decorative plant display, this book tells you everything you need to know. Learn which plants to keep in your home to purify the air and remove harmful chemicals and how to successfully grow plants from cacti to flowers to carnivorous plants.

Keeping Chickens for Beginners – Keeping Backyard Chickens from Coops to Feeding to Care and More

Chickens are becoming very popular to keep at home, but it isn't something you should leap into without the right information. This book guides you through everything you need to know to keep chickens from decided what breed to what coop to how to feed them, look after them and keep your chickens healthy and producing eggs. This is your complete guide to owning chickens, with absolutely everything you need to know to get started and successfully keep chickens at home.

Raised Bed Gardening – A Guide to Growing Vegetables In Raised Beds

Learn why raised beds are such an efficient and effortless way to garden as you discover the benefits of no-dig gardening, denser planting and less bending, ideal for anyone who hates weeding or suffers from back pain. Easy to build and lasting for years I cannot recommend this method of gardening enough for its many benefits! You will learn everything you need to know to build your own raised beds, plant them and ensure they are highly productive.

Save Our Bees – Your Guide to Creating a Bee Friendly Environment

Find out how you can help save the bees and protect this insect that is vital to your food production and environment. Our modern lives have disrupted the bees to a point where many are dying off. Learn what you can do to help the bees no matter how much space you have at home! Discover what bees need, how you can provide it and all about the different types of bees! These misunderstood creatures are harmless and fascinating insects.

Square Foot Gardening – Growing More in Less Space

Learn about this unique gardening style which enables you to grow more in less space. This dense planting method using nutrient rich soil to produce fantastic yields. You will learn exactly how to create your own square foot garden, how to create the perfect soil mix and exactly how to space your plants for maximum yields. You will find out what you can grow in a square foot garden as well as what to avoid growing plus helpful advice so you can make the most of your growing area. An in-depth guide to getting you started with your first square foot garden.

The Complete Allotment Guide - Volume 1 – Starting Out, Growing and Techniques: Everything You Need To Know To Grow Fruits and Vegetables

A complete guide to owning an allotment, but useful for anyone who wants to grow their own vegetables at home too. Detailing everything from how to get an allotment to allotment etiquette through to how to make your own compost, tackle weeds and more. This is the perfect book for the beginner or intermediate allotment owner with practical tips and advice from a long term allotment owner. Your first allotment can be very overwhelming, but this guide will help you turn a weedy patch into a productive vegetable garden. This guide is essential for anyone who has an allotment or is thinking about getting one, plus it will help any vegetable gardener grow more successfully.

Vertical Gardening: Maximum Productivity, Minimum Space

This is an exciting form of gardening allows you to grow large amounts of fruit and vegetables in small areas, maximizing your use of space. Whether you have a large garden, an allotment or just a small balcony, you will be able to grow more delicious fresh produce. Becoming more popular not just amongst gardeners but even with city planners, this is a fantastic gardening technique that significantly boosts your yield. Find out how I grew over 70 strawberry plants in just three feet of ground space and more in this detailed guide.

Worm Farming – Creating Compost at Home with Vermiculture

An in-depth guide to one of the hottest topics on the market as you learn how you can use worms to turn your kitchen scraps into a high quality, highly nutritious compost that will help your plants to thrive! Easy to set up, low cost and able to be done in a small corner of a shed or garage this is a fantastic way for anyone to make their own compost or even scale it up to create a highly profitable business. Discover how you can make one of the best composts on the market with kitchen waste and worms.

WANT MORE INSPIRING GARDENING IDEAS?

This book is part of the Inspiring Gardening Ideas series. Bringing you the best books anywhere on how to get the most from your garden or allotment. Please remember to leave a review on Amazon once you have finished this book as it helps me continually improve my books.

You can find out about more wonderful books just like this one at: www.GardeningWithJason.com

Follow me at www.YouTube.com/OwningAnAllotment for my video diary and tips. Join me on Facebook for regular updates and discussions at www.Facebook.com/OwningAnAllotment.

Find me on Instagram and Twitter as @allotmentowner where I post regular updates, offers and gardening news. Follow me today and let's catch up in person!

FREE BOOK!

Visit http://gardeningwithjason.com/your-free-book/ now for your free copy of my book "Environmentally Friendly Gardening" sent to your inbox. Discover today how you can become a more eco-friendly gardener and help us all make the world a better place.

This book is full of tips and advice, helping you to reduce your need for chemicals and work in harmony with nature to improve the environment. With the looming crisis, there is something we can all do in our gardens, no matter how big or small they are and they can still look fantastic!

Thank you for reading!

Lightning Source UK Ltd.
Milton Keynes UK
UKHW021316121222
413807UK00021B/433